GOOD LIFE, GOOD DEATH

Derek Humphry

2018

GOOD LIFE, GOOD DEATH

The Memoir of a Right to Die Pioneer

DEREK HUMPHRY

CARREL BOOKS

Carrel Books may be purchased in bulk at special discounts for sales promotion, corporate gifts, fund-raising, or educational purposes. Special editions can also be created to specifications. For details, contact the Special Sales Department, Carrel Books, 307 West 36th Street, 11th Floor, New York, NY 10018, or carrelbooks@skyhorsepublishing.com.

Carrel Books® is a registered trademark of Skyhorse Publishing, Inc.®, a Delaware corporation.

Visit our website at www.carrelbooks.com.

10 9 8 7 6 5 4 3 2 1

Library of Congress Cataloging-in-Publication Data is available on file.

Cover design by Rain Saukas
Cover photo credit: iStock

Print ISBN: 978-1-63144-066-3
Ebook ISBN: 978-1-63144-067-0

Printed in the United States of America

PRAISE FOR DEREK HUMPHRY

"Derek Humphry is widely acknowledged to be the initiator of the euthanasia reform movement in the United States."
—*Dying Right: The Death with Dignity Movement*
by Daniel Hillyard and John Dombrink

"If reporters could be cloned, I would clone Derek Humphry."
—Farewell to Humphry address by Harold Evans,
editor of the *London Sunday Times* (June 30, 1978)

"*Final Exit* is among the 25 most significant books published in the past quarter century."
—*USA Today* (April 2007)

To Gretchen:

My rock

CONTENTS

FOREWORD

D URING THE EARLY 1980s, after a university lecture on death and dying, a student brought me a newspaper clipping. It described a new organization that had been launched to focus on the right of terminally ill individuals to end their lives in a planned manner.

At the time I read the news clipping, the medical ethics community referred to the "right to die" almost solely as to the right of patients to craft living wills—legal documents in which one could specify in advance their desire to forego or remove unwanted life-sustaining measures.

This "right" was championed by the parents of twenty-one-year-old Karen Ann Quinlan. In April of 1975, Karen Ann suffered irreversible brain damage after mixing alcohol and valium at a party. They filed lawsuits to allow them to remove the ventilator they believed was keeping her alive. The next year, the New Jersey Supreme Court ruled on their behalf, citing that the right to privacy should encompass their request on Karen's behalf. Soon one state after another enacted legislation providing for such advance directives.

A month before Karen Ann Quinlan attended that fateful party, a husband and wife in Wiltshire, England, were facing a different type of decision. Jean Humphry was nearing the end of her long battle against metastasized breast cancer. Nine months earlier Jean's husband, Derek, had found a physician who agreed that Jean should have "insurance" should worse come to worse. The physician provided Derek with a lethal dose of medications that Jean could eventually use, if necessary, to end her life.

With the drugs in hand, Jean and Derek made a pact that she could take her life if the final weeks of suffering became unbearable, and if Derek agreed. Some nine months later, when the day finally arrived, Jean asked for the drugs, Derek mixed the medication in coffee, and gave it to her. She drank the mixture, and died within the hour.

Like many assisted deaths before and after, this one remained a secret. In 1978, however, Derek—a journalist for the *London Sunday Times* and award-winning author—published a book, *Jean's Way: A Love Story*, in which he described their life together and the course of her illness. He then detailed the factual circumstances of her death.

Jean's Way began a new "right to die" movement. The book became popular, first in England, then in Australia, and finally in the United States. In the media it garnered both intense criticism and support, and expanded the dialogue about assisted dying. As Derek describes in the following pages, it took him on a worldwide lecture tour, and in meeting or being contacted by countless people who confessed they had helped a loved one die or that they would want such help if it became necessary, the book set the stage for both a self-help movement and a call to legalize assisted dying—voluntary euthanasia and assisted suicide—as a choice for competent adults at the end of life.

At the time, no information was available on how one could end their life humanely or what medications they should use. With every new letter or plea for help Derek received, it became apparent to him that he could do something more, and after much thought he made the decision to create the Hemlock Society. The intention was not to encourage the terminally ill to end their lives but to educate them about the most humane ways to do so, and to promote public tolerance toward those who felt the need to make such a profound personal decision. In the long term, Hemlock also would fight to reform the laws to allow assisted death for the terminally ill. Organizational membership grew.

From the start, Derek promised that those who joined Hemlock would be given the information they could use if necessary. A new book, consisting of personal stories, would provide such. After expensive and time-consuming research, *Let Me Die Before I Wake* was made available, first to members and then the public.

Little did I know at the time, I would be strongly influenced by Derek's emphasis on research and requests for personal stories, which became the model I used much later to craft one of my own books.

A few years after that, I first read about the Hemlock Society; my sister was nearing the end of her own struggle with multiple sclerosis. As she was unable to communicate in any way other than a twitch of a finger or occasional tears, I never knew if she wanted to live or die. But sitting by her bedside, I finally understood why someone might want such a choice, and I also realized the anguish family members or friends face when thinking about helping another to die. These thoughts stayed with me.

After she died from pneumonia, and my father died by with-holding the medications he needed to live, I finally read *Let Me Die* and learned more about the Hemlock Society. I finally left the university and relocated nearby to the San Francisco Bay Area. My goal was to follow my passion to lecture and run work-shops and facilitate support groups on various end-of-life issues.

At the time, the AIDS epidemic was skyrocketing in San Francisco. Death had become far too common, and the city had become a human slaughterhouse. The gaunt faces of those who would soon be dead could be seen on every street corner in the Castro.

One day, a workshop attendee invited me to the grand open-ing of an AIDS daycare facility run by a friend of hers. The director was also the president of the San Francisco chapter of Hemlock. She asked about my work and then asked me if I'd like to facilitate a support group for Hemlock Society members, most of whom were dying from AIDS. I agreed.

A few months later, two of my Hemlock support group mem-bers asked me to join them at a presentation by Derek Hum-phry and Ron Adkins. Mr. Adkins was the widowed husband of Janet Adkins, the first person to use Dr. Jack Kevorkian's "sui-cide machine." Derek described the need for new laws, and how San Francisco—the epicenter of the AIDS epidemic—showed the obvious need for such change. And Mr. Adkins described how his wife, Janet, died on a cot in the back of Dr. Kevorkian's Volkswagen van. When asked why this couldn't be carried out in a more dignified location, he quickly responded by saying that society had placed Janet in that van.

At the next support group meeting, the members were excited. More than one saw Dr. Kevorkian as a hero. I disagreed, but remained quiet. There needed to be a better way. I felt a person should be able to die at home, surrounded by those they loved. As it was, people were being helped—every day. In the face of the epidemic, physicians in larger numbers were helping, but were doing so secretly, with a wink and a nod, most often without adequate discussion and often haphazardly with the wrong drugs. And patients were helping each other by putting together "drug kits" composed of leftover medications, hoping they would work.

A few months after his presentation, I finally met Derek Humphry and discussed with him possible ways to help build the organization in California. We would open a San Francisco office, engage in outreach to help secure California funds for a Washington State ballot campaign, and lay the groundwork for a similar future campaign in California.

After securing a storefront office, we set up shop. With several dedicated volunteers I organized and staffed a large number of events across the region and then took up the task of media and public outreach in an effort to help build membership through public awareness.

Soon, however, any potential difficulties in promoting Hemlock in the media and building its membership were swept away as the movement took on its own life. It was a case of my being at the right place at the right time.

In 1991, the Washington initiative had made the ballot, and Derek asked me to arrange a speaking and fund-raising tour in northern California. He would discuss the ballot measure, and, hopefully, we would obtain donations for the campaign. In preparation, Derek shipped me several boxes of a new book, which we would try to sell at these events.

Derek had recently secured publication of *Final Exit*, a how-to book on self-deliverance. Hemlock members were made aware of his tour through mailings and were excited to hear him speak and to purchase the book, which was unavailable in stores. As he describes in the following pages, the book languished until a well-placed article about it brought international attention. The article coincided with the speaking tour. I remember waiting for him outside a phone booth in Carmel while he discussed with his publisher the need to immediately engage a massive new printing. While on this tour, the book went to the top of the *New York Times* nonfiction best-sellers list, and lines formed at every event to purchase signed copies.

We couldn't sell books or sign up new members fast enough. Nor did I have to work too hard to secure radio or television interviews for Derek or me. Calls came in daily with requests from national shows to send "dying patients" to the national shows back in New York. The producers preferred young women with cancer, but would accept AIDS patients—if they were the only ones available. I provided whomever I could who supported the cause and was willing to speak publicly about their desire for an assisted death.

The media attention continued to build, as supporters soon launched their own signature campaign. The initiative qualified for the 1992 ballot, but in California, as in Washington State, the ballots were both defeated. Throughout all this, Derek was stoic and told me at the time it may take twenty years, but that at each step we'd get closer. As in most of his political observations, he was right.

Meanwhile, I continued to facilitate my groups in San Francisco. And I listened as members discussed their symptoms and quality of life, the inevitability of their deaths, their now-dead friends, and their aborted plans for the future. But most importantly, the topic always turned back to their imminent deaths, and the groups became a safety valve where they could discuss their concerns or plans without fear or judgment.

Each week there would be stories—stories of friends who had died badly, and others who had wanted an assisted death but who had failed to secure the right medication, had become physically or mentally unable to take matters into their own hands, or were now dependent on caregivers who vehemently disagreed with their preferred choice. These stories inspired comments like "I'll never wait that long" or "I'll end it while I can still think clearly" or "I'll never share my plans with my family." They would talk about getting their drug kits together, or about asking their physicians for the right prescription. *Final Exit* was their bible.

Within two years, all the original members of the groups were dead, some from natural causes but more who had been aided in their dying by others. According to those friends, partners, or family members with whom I talked (some of whom had also attended my groups), most of these deaths were positive. But others were less so because they were shrouded in secrecy or lacked the best means to die. Some died alone. Others were discovered in progress and rushed to the hospital.

Of those who helped, most saw their involvement as an act of love. But there were others who experienced post-traumatic stress. In one case an impatient father used a plastic bag after his son lapsed into unconsciousness. He was afraid the drugs might not work and didn't want his son to wake. Another member met a similar fate when the person who agreed to be there for support became afraid that time was running out and, if he waited any longer, he would be seen by the member's roommate when she got home.

These stories and countless others I heard during that time, sparked the idea to engage in research similar to what Derek engaged in years earlier.

As a result, I asked for and received Derek's support to place an ad in the *Hemlock Quarterly* requesting interviews with those who had participated in an assisted death. I wanted to hear about both good and bad deaths as well as what the effects had been on them personally. I received countless responses, phone calls, letters, and postcards, and conducted over two hundred interviews. This resulted in my writing and publishing *Final Acts of Love* as well as a second volume for physicians. Without Derek's nurturance, none of that would have happened.

Over the years, Hemlock vanished through name changes and mergers. Nevertheless, it set the stage for the legal changes that have taken place. This, of course, began with the successful ballot measure legalizing assisted dying in Oregon in 1994, then again in 1997, as well as in a ballot measure passed in Washington State in 2008. The next year, the highest court in Montana ruled that physicians are authorized under state law to prescribe medication that terminally ill adults can take to shorten their dying process if suffering becomes unbearable. And finally, in 2015, legislative action resulted in similar legislation being signed into law in both Vermont and California. Similar legislation is in the works elsewhere.

What I've discovered in my work and research, and what's been discovered in those states where assisted dying has been legalized, is that most terminally ill do not end their lives when they secure a potentially lethal prescription. Like Jean Humphry, when a person knows they have a choice available to them, they can choose to live one more day, and then one more.

None of these changes would have occurred without the work of Derek Humphry, beginning with his first books and lectures, his decision to devote himself full-time to establishing and growing the Hemlock Society, authoring his groundbreaking volume, *Final Exit*, and continuing to educate the public and health professionals about this vital additional choice to help the dying.

—Stephen Jamison, PhD
California, February 2016

Stephen Jamison, PhD, is a social psychologist, medical ethicist, and author. He received his doctorate from the University of California, Davis, where he also served on the faculty for several years and was responsible for teaching courses that included death and dying, social psychology, and family.

Dr. Jamison educates healthcare professionals on communication issues around end-of-life medical decisions. He is the author of numerous articles and books on end-of-life issues and the resolution of family conflict in healthcare decisions. His books include *Final Acts of Love* (Tarcher/Putnam-Penguin Publishing, 1996) and *Assisted Suicide: A Decision-Making Guide for Health Professionals* (Jossey-Bass, 1997).

He has served on hospital ethics committees and the Advisory Committee on End-of-Life Decisions of the American Psychological Association and was president of the Mental Health Association of Marin County. In addition, he worked as regional director of the Hemlock Society, executive director of the World Federation of Right to Die Societies, and California coordinator for Compassion & Choices, and was director of the Aid-in-Dying Communication Project of the San Francisco Medical Society Community Education Foundation.

PREFACE

WHEN I WAS FORTY-EIGHT I decided to desert my native England and spend the second half of my life in America. Despite a slender wartime education, I had climbed from messenger boy to the top of English journalism with the *Sunday Times*, published four books, won a literary prize, raised a family, and was settled in London.

But the appeal of America, its variety and hugeness, its riches and poverty, its brilliance and its darkness, all greatly appealed to me. I had exhausted the best of little England. (With my second wife a US citizen, I had no trouble with immigration rules.)

Thirty years after flying west to join the *Los Angeles Times*, I do not regret my chosen relocation, though my spell at that newspaper was short yet highly productive. Not realized by me at the time, the worldwide publication of *Jean's Way*, a memoir of how I helped my first wife die to escape the last ravages of terminal cancer, was changing the whole course of my life.

As I relate in this book, events caused me to found the Hemlock Society USA in my garage in Santa Monica, kick-start the

American right to die movement, and self-publish perhaps the most controversial nonfiction book ever to hit the number one spot on *The New York Times* best-seller list: *Final Exit*. I began campaigning for the Oregon physician-assisted suicide law eight years before it was eventually passed. For ten years it remained the only such law in the US.

Ten years after I started the Hemlock Society, Dr. Jack Kevorkian arrived, but we never hit it off, even though fundamentally we were driving down the same track, seeking to allow all people who had enjoyed a good life to then achieve a good death. This is a memoir of the important events in my life, not an autobiography. So many happenings in my life were to have consequences much later on that a linear sequence of events is nearly impossible.

—Derek Humphry

GOOD LIFE, GOOD DEATH

Introduction

LIFE AFTER DEATH

Back when I was chief editor of the *Havering Recorder*, a weekly tabloid newspaper in Greater London, I was sitting at my desk one Friday morning, admiring the week's work in print of my team and me, when the telephone rang.

"Is this the editor?"

"Speaking."

"It says on the front page of your newspaper that I'm dead."

Ouch! I grabbed the paper. There on the front page was a brief news item naming a man who had collapsed and died in a city street.

"Is this you?" I asked the caller.

"It's me, but I ain't dead yet."

This was about the worst blunder a newspaper can make. Not only did it reek of inefficiency, but can there be a worse libel than stating a person is dead when they are not? A smart lawyer might take us for everything we owned.

I asked the caller to stay put and I would be with him shortly. I jumped in my car and tore around to his house. There I found an elderly couple at the kitchen table beside the remains of an abandoned breakfast, my newspaper thrown to one side. I apologized profusely for our error and then, seeking to blunt any possible verbal attack, quickly asked how they found out about the "death." They offered me a chair and a cup of tea, seemingly anxious to tell someone. This was the story they told me.

Every Friday morning a man came to clean their windows, regularly giving a wave as he mounted his ladder to clean the upstairs panes. That morning, when he was halfway up, he froze, dropping his bucket, staring transfixed at the breakfasting couple. His paralysis continued so long that the couple went outside and asked him if something was wrong.

"It says in the paper that you're dead," said the window cleaner. "I thought I was seeing a ghost."

"Well, you can see I'm not dead," said the man, who then rushed indoors to get the paper and read that what the window cleaner had said was true, insofar as what was printed. Then he called me. Around the dining room table, we talked about the incident, and other local news, for an hour or so. By the time I left we were friends. Back at the office, I called in the young reporter who had blundered. We traced that while checking his facts, he had read the wrong name and address from a street directory. Another error like that, I told him, and you're fired. The following week I printed a correction on the front page; that was the last I heard of the matter. I was fortunate that the couple were so forgiving.

Stories of dying and death normally scream at us from television and newspaper headlines. It's the attention-getter the media must have. My life, both in and out of journalism, has had a great deal to do with death, but none ended as pleasantly as the man who discovered life after (reported) death.

Chapter 1

A Shaky Start

T HIS EVENTFUL LIFE FOR me began in Bath, Somerset, England, on April 29, 1930. My father, a traveling salesman, was renting a two-room apartment on the second floor of a four-story Victorian row house, 3 Belvedere Villas, on the steeply sloping Lansdowne Road, in this elegant Roman and Georgian city. There he had temporarily installed my mother and my older brother Garth, then two years old. Bath was the grandiose background to Jane Austen's novels, and the handsome movies of her stories made in the city, but our family's life was much more mundane and shaky.

I do not owe my parents much beyond the act of procreation and early succoring. The few facts I know about my mother, Bettine Elizabeth Duggan, are that she was born in Athlone, County Westmeath, Ireland, in 1910, to racehorse trainer James Duggan and a Belgian woman, Charmaine De Silva. She had, so I heard, been brought up in Roman Catholic convents in Ireland and Belgium. That was the extent of the information I ever knew of that side of the family. A few faded snapshots of her taken in the 1930s show a tall, slim, dark-haired woman with sharply molded features. Old photos show a carefully groomed and elegantly dressed woman, a description that fits the rumor that she was both a nightclub hostess and fashion model in London when she met and married my father in 1927.

Many people try to spell my name as Humphrey, which is the generally common way. It comes from Middle English, of Germanic origin, introduced into England by the Normans in 1066. It has been used over the last one thousand years both as a first and a last name. There are thirteen known variations of its spelling in modern times, chiefly because in olden days the parish registers were kept by the only literate person in the village, the priest, and he often accidentally changed the spelling or it was misread by others. Anyway, for many generations, my family has consistently spelled it Humphry without an "e" or any of the other ways. When people have taxed me about using this rarer form of spelling, I've countered that Humphry is the shorter, thus a more convenient, mode.

My father, Royston Humphry, was born in 1903 to a Bristol couple, the second of their four children. The Humphrys were pillars of middle-class respectability and were upwardly mobile. My grandfather, Ernest Humphry, was a Somerset country boy who moved into the city to fight his way up to become area sales manager of the North British Rubber Company. He was a prominent Freemason, in 1940 becoming Worshipful Master of Bristol lodge. They expected their children to emulate them. All but my father succeeded. Roy was the black sheep of the family, always in financial trouble, forever shocking people with his outrageous lifestyle and heretical views. After winning a scholarship to one of the best schools in Bristol, he was expelled for misbehavior. He gave up on job after job as too boring and then plunged into the maelstrom of crazy life in London in the 1920s with gusto. This was his ideal world—fast and wild with the promises of easy riches. He drank until his eyes nearly popped out of their sockets, and his large nose (which I have inherited) turned permanently lumpy and bright red, not unlike that of W. C. Fields. He had lost a piece of a front tooth in a fight, replacing it with a gold chip, which was rather cute. He drove fast cars—chiefly Studebakers and Railtons—and chased women relentlessly. Good-looking, charming, and personable, I heard him described—even by his detractors—as "perhaps England's finest salesman, able to sell anything to anyone."

Nowadays, a wild couple like my parents would probably practice birth control, or abortion, to avoid childbearing until their marriage either cemented or cracked up. In those days, however, knowledge and availability of birth control methods were both taboo and rudimentary, so my brother and I arrived within the first two years of their marriage. There was no fixed home, no steady job, and both Father and Mother loved to dance and drink all night. In mitigation, I should point out that they were not unusual for their time. Both were high-spirited people caught up in the "live for today" lifestyle so common in the 1920s and 1930s. Between the two genocidal world wars it was fashionable—perhaps logical—to "live for the moment."

The instability of this union is shown by Mother's action in 1930. The three-year-old marriage, with one two-year-old child already, saw my mother flee the home and board a cargo ship bound for India. She was heavily pregnant with me, thus as soon as the captain realized that he would be dealing with childbirth on the high seas—without a doctor or nurse—when he refueled in Gibraltar, he had her taken off and put on a ship back to England. A few weeks, later I was born in an apartment in Bath. Soon after, the marriage broke up, with divorce proceedings following. Despite their appalling records as parents, each fought furiously for custody of Garth and me.

For a couple of years, Garth and I lived most exciting lives, although hardly conducive to family values and sound education. As a typical example, I have vague, leftover impressions that we would be walking along a street in Bristol when a taxi would draw up alongside and Mother would beckon us over. Once inside the cab, there would be hugs and kisses and Mother would say something like: "I'm taking you on a trip. Don't worry. It's okay." There would follow a hundred-mile dash to London either in the cab or by train, depending on Mother's current financial situation. Once in the great city, we would be hidden in a small apartment with nothing else to do but play and read. We were never allowed out. Mother had to earn a living, of course, so at night we were left to ourselves.

Meantime, Father would have employed a private detective to trace our whereabouts, and within a few weeks we would be located. The kidnap scenario would be reversed: Father would pull up in one of his big American cars (never paid for, apparently), get into the apartment while Mother was working, and off we would race back to our other life in Bristol.

I do not remember very much of these snatches happening to me because I was only between two and five at the time. Garth and my aunts told me about these events over subsequent years. I do have faint memories of the car dashes between London and Bristol, but I wasn't sure what all the commotion was about—which was probably merciful. I recall hours spent staring out of windows at city streets, watching other children at play or with their parents, not understanding that I was a pawn and a prisoner of a crazy war over custody. Childlike, I assumed that everybody's lives were a constant push-and-pull between people who lived in lots of different homes between which they commuted at ridiculous speeds and at great expense!

For my older brother it was much more painful. I came to realize in my adulthood that our nomadic childhood experiences had permanently scarred him psychologically. Two years older, and very bright, Garth must have known exactly what was behind the antics going on and suffered appallingly. He grew up a somewhat arrogant man, touchy and tetchy. Although intelligent and extremely well read, he had trouble in achieving any of his ambitions. His first two marriages proved desperately unhappy; fortunately the third union worked, and it was not until he was in his fifties that he had fewer personal stresses and began to prosper financially.

Garth became my substitute father and mother between the ages of two and thirteen. He was most valuable at shielding me from the vicissitudes of those mobile and angry years. It did not matter a lot that our parents were hopeless, because Garth was always there to protect me. At the same time, I expect it gave him a mission, a purpose in life. Using his powerful imagination, already bolstered by extensive reading, Garth spun a fantasy world of words for the two of us. We played a game of two children who enjoyed a domain of their own with no adults present. Somewhat like the African slaves to the New World who devised their own language so that the white master could not overhear their conversations, we devised special words and phrases that only we understood. We gave ourselves new names—mine was "Tiddler," after the little fish, because I was so small. Alone by day and far into the night in the safety of our beds, we imagined and verbalized splendid adventures: fighting battles on the high seas, parachuting in the nick of time from crashing aircraft, and waging titanic struggles between armies of which we were the undisputed generals.

In the mid-1930s my father and mother fought bitterly in the divorce courts for custody of us. Coming from a solid, middle-class family, Roy was able to employ better legal services. My middle-class grandparents also appeared to offer us a stable home. The courts naturally came down on Father's side. Crushed by the defeat, Mother contracted a hasty marriage with a man called Wills, fled from Britain, and started a new life in Australia. My father's family, cocky and victorious, constantly informed Garth and me that Mother was "no-good," had "abandoned us," and was not worth thinking about. Because of this brainwashing and because I was so young at the time, I grew up without any idea of what Bettine even looked like. But I never really swallowed the story about her running away from us. Even at that impressionable age I preferred to wait, find out the facts, and then judge for myself.

Cared for by loving grandparents, our lives settled down for the first time, and I attended a junior school (grades nine through twelve) regularly. Grandfather had a stern, controlling manner, whereas Grandmother was sweet and warm—but always shrewd. She arranged a nanny for Garth and me, easing the workload of looking after two lively boys. As a salesman, Father traveled all the time, and he had several love affairs going on in London (one with a well-known actress of the day). But some Sundays he would come back to see his sons, and there is no doubt in my mind that he loved us.

Our calm existence lasted only one year. I went off to Cub camp for a week (Cubs are a junior version of Boy Scouts) and I returned to chaos. Grandmother had been taken ill and suddenly died at the age of sixty-one. She had contracted severe septicemia in her throat in an age when there were no antibiotics and choked to death within days. Ten years later, penicillin would have saved her. With the "earth mother" of the Humphry family gone, Grandfather was absolutely shattered and closed up his home. My aunts and uncles were all deeply involved with their own early careers, new marriages, and children. Father was permanently absent; Garth and I were stranded. Nobody knew what to do with us.

The solution arrived at was to alternate us between all the family homes. We would spend one month at a time in each of three different places. That way, it was reckoned, we would not be an excessive burden on anybody.

The resulting lifestyle taught me early on to respect dates and schedules and to be punctual. On the first day of each month, Garth and I packed our suitcases and went to a different house. Only seven years old, I dreaded forgetting the switchover date or turning up at the wrong house, which I sometimes did and got scolded. To handle the scheduling problem, I memorized a little rhyme that I happened upon:

Thirty days hath September, April, June, and November
All the rest have thirty-one
Excepting February alone
Which has twenty-eight days clear
And twenty-nine in each Leap Year

Aided by the dates on newspapers, this rhyme guided me so that I did not overstay my welcome and get scolded. Not that my aunts and uncles were at all unkind; they did their best to succor the two stray kids. But their young lives were full. Moreover, they resented Roy's total abandonment of his responsibilities. One day I left school at the end of the day's lessons badly in need of a bowel movement. I thought I could hold on until I reached my current "home." I arrived at Aunt Gwen's door but was told politely that I had made a mistake and come to the wrong place.

Ashamed of my carelessness, I made haste to Aunt Ena's, which was about a mile away, but as I ran, my bowels began to move on the city street! To my mortification, the excrement began to fall from my shorts onto the sidewalk. I felt that the whole world was watching my disgusting behavior and was repulsed by this little boy who was not even toilet trained.

My anger at this humiliation ran so deep, it must have been then that the seeds of my independence were sown. I realized that I needed to take control of my own life and not rely on other people—with the exception of Garth, my only support.

Of course, while this nomadic life was unsettling, to a certain degree it was not without many happy moments. Father—when he appeared—lavished love and toys on us. Relatives, trying to compensate, took Garth and me to the circus, the pantomime, and the seaside, just like other middle-class families. Compared to millions of other children in the world, Garth and I were pampered. The Depression era had passed as the 1930s wore on, and the whole family was doing fairly well economically.

Eventually, the "family committee" realized that the monthly transfer among homes was unsatisfactory; it's possible that a coincidental tragedy influenced events more than I knew at the time.

Aunt Gwen's first baby, Michael, was eighteen months old when he contracted pneumonia and would later die. I was seven. Unfortunately, it was my turn to stay at her home when he first took ill, and I had caught the measles at school. I quickly got over the minor disease. Very soon after Michael's death I went into my aunt's bedroom to take her a cup of tea. She was prostrate with grief. Demented, she suddenly sat up in bed and screamed at me: "You killed my baby! Get out! You killed my baby!"

Horrified, I rushed downstairs. My shocked countenance must have alarmed Gwen's husband, Harry, a kind and intelligent

man. He asked me what was wrong. I told him what had happened upstairs.

"How could I have killed Michael?" I begged. "I loved him."

Uncle Harry sat down with me and explained that I had
brought home the measles infection from school, which Michael
contracted on top of his pneumonia. The doctor had told Aunt
Gwen that the combined illnesses had killed her baby. With
extraordinary patience and tact, Uncle Harry explained to me that
this was how life sometimes worked—cause and effect—in this
case, it was disastrous. Although I had contributed to Michael's
death, it was totally accidental. I was not to blame myself. Uncle
Harry explained that he did not hold me responsible and that he
did not think Aunt Gwen would either once she had recovered
from her terrible anguish and despair.

"You will learn, Derek, that in life people say many things that
they don't really mean," I recall Uncle Harry saying. "Things are
said in the heat of the moment which we later regret. The secret
is to remain calm over time and try to judge for oneself the truth
of a situation."

Aunt Gwen recovered and later gave birth to another child,
Christopher. She never again reproached me about Michael. I
doubt if she even remembered her crazed accusation. Until she
died at the age of ninety, she was one of my best friends and
supporters. There was real affection between us, and we kept in
touch even when separated by thousands of miles. I wept at her
funeral fifty-four years after Michael's death.

The story of Michael's death, of course, left a lasting impression on me. First, as Uncle Harry had wisely pointed out, never
rush to take literally what people shout in anger. More significantly, bad things happen in life that are nobody's direct fault
even though one might be involved. It struck me pretty forcibly, after all that had happened to me in my first eight years,

that everybody—other than babies in need of care—must take
responsibility for their own lives. This was a harsh philosophy,
perhaps, at so tender an age, but necessary. Between periods of
happiness there were more trials to come.

Not long after this, Uncle Harry saved my life.

I was always "weak chested" as it was called in the 1930s. A
bout of influenza turned into pneumonia and, in the days before
antibiotics, this was often a killer. One night I was so ill the doctor warned that if I went to sleep, my lungs would collapse and
I would die. So Uncle Harry sat up all night talking to me and
keeping me from sleeping. I dimly remember that as dawn came
up I extracted a promise from him.

"Please, I want a bus conductor's outfit," I implored. At that
point I considered this the most glamorous, worthwhile job in
the world. Later that day he brought me the uniform, cap, tick-
ets, and ticket punch, and I was on the road to recovery.

Uncle Harry, whose shriveled legs due to polio were held
together by hinged steel braces, was in effect my father from the
ages of five through nine. Still a boy at heart, he built an elaborate model railway train track set that ran between the bushes, up
and down the garden. On summer Sunday mornings, we would
spend hours with him playing with this wonderful toy. Model
railways were a boy's principal toy in the 1930s. Our train set,
thanks to Harry's money and technical brilliance as a professional
watch and clock repairer, was the envy of the neighborhood.

I treasure a photograph of Harry sitting beside a little wig-
wam in the garden, stripped to the waist, wearing an Indian head-
band, with Garth and me dressed as cowboys. Garth and I also
collected toy soldiers made of lead, and we would arrange them
across the living room carpet in mock battles. One day Harry
came into the room with something bulging under his sweater.
Because he was obliged to walk with two sticks, he often carried

articles tucked into his clothes, and I thought that this was merely a clock or something he was going to repair. He flopped down on the carpet and clicked his leg calipers into the folding position, watching our war game keenly. At a crucial moment during our "war" he reached under his sweater and pulled out a toy cannon on wheels that ejected wooden shells. He proceeded to "shoot us all down" with great gusto. That's how I remember Harry, as a man who adored children and was hugely generous to me. When the real war came, he was ordered into military aircraft production as an instrument repairer. The constant moves around the country led to the breakup of his marriage to Gwen, so he never had the pleasure of raising his second son, Christopher, born two years after Michael's death.

While the general pattern of my first ten years was of broken homes, changing schools, and a complete absence of parental care and affection, it would be a mistake to think that I was unhappy. Glancing through snapshot albums reminds me of the scores of visits to the seaside– Weston-super-Mare (we children called it "Weston Super Mud") and the more pleasant Somerset resorts of Portishead and Clevedon. Given the economic harshness of the 1930s, I enjoyed an average middle-class upbringing, with motorcars to take me on trips and pocket money for toys and candy.

Because of the transfer of infection that contributed to Michael's death, and for another as yet unrevealed reason, the family became more concerned about our rootlessness. It was agreed that in the future I would live permanently with Aunt Stella, and Garth would reside with Aunt Gwen. We were even asked if this was agreeable. It was fine by the two of us, for our new permanent homes were about a mile apart on the Wells Road, Knowle. Ours was a close family, and we went to the same school. Now that I was eight, Garth did not need to protect me as much. We concluded playing those fantasy games that had been so important to my emotional survival.

Father seemed to still be living the high life in London. I regularly wrote him childish notes that Uncle Harry mailed, after writing out another envelope into which he put my letter. I childishly assumed that this was because my handwriting was so poor that the mailman could not understand it. Why I should be writing to my father instead of seeing him puzzled me. I found out many years later.

Aunt Stella did not have her own two children until some years later, so I was treated like a son. For my ninth birthday she threw a tremendous party, and I was allowed to invite all my playmates. There were lashings of ice cream, jelly, blancmange, and fizzy lemonade. Stella and my blood uncle, Horace, owned a large stone house on the Wells Road. There, they gave over two empty rooms to us kids, where we could gorge ourselves senseless and act crazily without damaging anything. After the delicacies were scoffed, we wrestled and boxed and generally— as Uncle Horace loved to describe it afterwards—"went crackers." I enjoyed a superbly happy year with Aunt Stella and Uncle Horace, compensating hugely for the difficult past years. At nine, a boy doesn't care that much about not having real parents so long as the lemonade, candy, and chocolates keep coming, and the people around him are not shouting at each other.

From an early age, I was always keenly aware of world events, probably because the people with whom I lived always read newspapers, listened to the radio, and argued about political affairs. Someone named Hitler was seizing other countries in Europe. I gathered from the adult conversations that if he was not stopped, little England would be next. In 1938 there was the "Munich crisis," and our prime minister, Neville Chamberlain, barely forestalled an immediate war. He was heavily criticized at the time for appeasement. History has shown, however, that Chamberlain was stalling for time while England re-armed for war. But another argument says that if England and France had forcibly checked Hitler earlier, when he was militarily weak, World War II would not have happened.

The imminence of war was sharply brought home to me when my father, whom I had not seen in about two years, suddenly appeared one day wearing the blue uniform of the Royal Air Force. On his left chest was a badge with one wing, and the letters "AG."

"What's AG mean, Dad?" I asked.

"Air Gunner," he replied.

"I'm the rear gunner in a Blenheim bomber ready for when the war comes."

Proud for once of my father, I boasted about this to the kids at school, none of whose fathers were yet in the armed services. One boy—sharper, better informed, and more outspoken than the others—commented:

"Your dad's a 'Tail End Charlie.' It's the most dangerous job in the air force. They get hit first when the fighters attack from behind. He must be suicidal!" To make things a little more optimistic, the boy added: "I hope he's a good shot and gets them first."

"He's been well trained." That was all I could think to respond to this shattering analysis. After all, why was my father, one of the confirmed playboys of London, acting so bravely? He had never shown any jingoistic traits. He loved life far too much to ever contemplate suicide. I was not to learn the answer until after the war.

One Sunday morning in September 1939, after breakfast, the radio was turned on. There was an air of anxious expectancy in the household. In sonorous tones, the prime minister announced that as Germany had refused to withdraw its invasion

troops from Poland. "This country is now at war," he declared.
Although only nine, I was horror-struck. I had read a good deal
about the terrible bloodshed of World War I, which had ended a
mere twenty-one years earlier. I assumed this would be a repeat
of that catastrophe and that my father would be among the first
to die.

When Uncle Horace asked me if I realized that we were now
at war, I was in such a state of shock I was unable to speak. "He's
too young to understand," Horace scoffed, making the oft-
repeated error of adults of underestimating the savvy of children.

Life during the so-called "phony war" went on without change
for nearly a year. Then Nazi Germany struck into Belgium and
France, and the Allies were driven out. Much of the British army
managed to escape, though without guns or equipment, through
a sea rescue armada via Dunkirk. But in 1940 things looked
pretty grim for England. Millions were, like me, encouraged by
Winston Churchill's booming "We shall never surrender" pronouncement and other heartening statements over the radio, but
the impact of the war began to be felt in several respects.

British lightweight bombers, the Blenheim squadrons in
which Father served, began to bomb Berlin nightly and drop
propaganda leaflets on Hamburg. Why Hamburg was selected
for the leaflets defied the public's comprehension. A children's
joke at the time went: "Why do we drop leaflets only on Hamburg? Because they're the only Germans who can read!" It was
part of the defensive humor that kids under stress employed to
keep up their spirits. For instance, in the playground we used to
chant this ditty in 1941:

What a surprise for the Duce,
He can't put it over the Greeks.

Hitler has only one ball,
But Mussolini has no balls at all.

I expect German and Italian children at the same time had similar humor mocking Winston Churchill and Franklin Roosevelt.

I listened to the daily BBC news bulletins with apprehension for any change in the expected announcement: "Last night our bombers attacked military and naval targets in Germany. All of our aircraft returned safely." Later the bulletins began to vary somewhat, adding a chilling final sentence, which later became the title of a famous movie: "One of our aircraft is missing."

Then came word that Father was in a hospital with leg wounds. Coming back from an attack over Hamburg, his Blenheim was attacked by Messerschmitt fighters and badly damaged. Father received numerous bullet wounds to his legs but fortunately not to his body or head. His pilot escaped the enemy fighters over the English Channel by dropping to sea level and skimming home over the tops of the waves, and making a forced landing in a wheat field in Kent.

When he came out of the hospital, Father was as happy as a dog with two tails. He had fought for his country, been wounded, "done his bit" as they said, and now confidently looked forward to an early discharge from the air force. But to his great disappointment, he was graded unfit for flying duties and he returned to active ground duty. Although his legs had healed well, they would not hold up to a parachute landing, which aircrew might have to make.

The Battle of Britain between the Royal Air Force and the Luftwaffe for the control of the skies was in full swing. Father was put in charge of a machine gun on the white cliffs of Dover with orders to shoot down Stukas as they dive-bombed the harbor.

He spent the summer of 1940 on the front line and fired thousands of rounds into the air, though he never bagged a Stuka. I
do recall seeing a newspaper group photograph of him and five
other RAF men who were credited in the caption with shooting
down a German fighter with a burst of rifle fire. If true, it must
have been one of the war's greatest flukes! Normally a boastful
man, Father told me that he was never sure that the six riflemen
had actually downed the plane, though it did crash. It was great
morale-boosting wartime publicity.

At night the Germans hurled heavy shells across a twenty-
mile stretch of the English Channel, trying to pulverize Dover
and demoralize England. At the same time hundreds of German bombers were devastating British cities. In Dover, both the
servicemen and the remaining inhabitants—most had previously
been evacuated—sheltered in the deep caves under the cliffs. In
one of these caves, Father met a woman who was to change his
life.

Sybil was raven-haired, good-looking, tall, willowy, well
groomed, and about thirty, a few years older than Dad. She and
Father fell madly in love and, as best they could in war-torn
Dover, began to live together. Nowadays such conduct is fairly
normal but it was quite unusual back then. What was not unusual
were the appalling tensions that people on the front line faced—a
bomb or a shell "with their names on it" as they say, could wipe
them off the face of the earth at any second. So men and women
clutched at basic emotions and the fulfillment of life without
thought for customs or traditions. It was a society under siege
with a "live now, pay later" attitude. Under such circumstances
it's common for the sex urge to be considerably heightened. So, it
was no surprise that a love child was conceived by Roy and Sybil.
It should have been a happy event, but the prospect of marriage
was a terribly serious matter for both of them. Father was in bad

favor with his whole family, not only over his divorce, but for dumping Garth and me on his brothers and sisters. He was also heavily in debt to his father for costs of the lengthy divorce and custody proceedings. News of yet another hasty marriage would, he knew, incur the wrath of the whole family.

For her part, Sybil had always been warned by her parents not to marry, claiming that if she did she would soon die of tuberculosis. They based this on the history of previous generations of their family. So when Sybil told them that she was pregnant by a man whom she loved deeply, they were shocked but powerless. Roy and Sybil were secretly married in 1941. A daughter, Beverley Ann, was soon born, but Roy kept the whole thing from his sons and the rest of his family for two years.

The couple was very much in love, and the baby was adored. It looked as though this would be a truly happy union. As the Battle of Britain finished, with England narrowly victorious, Roy was transferred from the cliff top machine gun nest to the operations room of an RAF Command base in Kent. This meant he could ride out the rest of the war in an important yet safe job.

But the Damoclean sword that had hung over the lovely Sybil all her life now fell with a vengeance. The parental prediction turned out to be true: Sybil developed what was then called "galloping consumption" and was soon "terminal." Poor Roy was under enormous strain, with his war tasks, a dying wife, a baby, and her parents blaming him for the calamity. The latter was certainly unfair. Sybil had decided to live life to the fullest and to take her chances, enjoying married love and motherhood whatever the risk.

In desperation, Father returned to Bristol in 1943 and threw himself on the mercy of his family. They did not fail him. It was then that I learned I'd had a stepmother for the past two years and a half sister. Aunt Gwen took the baby into her care so that

Sybil could enter a tuberculosis sanatorium in an eleventh hour attempt to save her life. I remember one occasion when Father got compassionate leave. Together, he and I cycled the fifteen miles to the sanatorium to visit her. It was one of the rare occasions when I spent quality time with him. I can still recall the sight of their great love as she lay emaciated in the sanatorium bed, bravely trying to be upbeat and purposeful. On other occasions, when he could borrow a car and obtain rationed gasoline, father would take baby Beverley to the fence surrounding the sanatorium. He'd hold up the child so that her mother could fleetingly see her from her bed on an outdoor veranda. Children's visits were not allowed for fear of TB infection. This pathetic over-the-fence visiting arrangement has always haunted me.

Father begged the RAF for a compassionate discharge, but such was the shortage of manpower in 1944 that he was refused. Britain had no reserves to replace serious manpower losses in the invasion of France.

When she was finally pronounced hopeless by the doctors, Sybil returned to her parents' home in Kent to die. At least she was near her husband's base. Every day, stressed out and barely holding on, Roy spent twelve hours on duty in the Operations Room and twelve more with his wife. She gradually slipped downhill, and in late 1944 she died. Within the next five years, the antibiotics that would probably have saved her life were brought into common medical use.

My brother and I insisted on attending her funeral. This meant traveling from the relatively safe haven of Somerset some two hundred miles to less-secure Kent. The Germans were making a last-ditch effort to win the war by launching thousands of V1 and V2 rockets with explosive warheads at London and southeast England. The day before we boarded the train from London to Canterbury, where Sybil was to be buried, a German fighter-bomber had strafed a train on the same line. But Garth and I were oddly determined to be at that funeral despite the German attacks. We heard V2 rocket missiles—which we called "buzz-bombs"—flying overhead, but none landed near us.

I hardly knew my stepmother and could not grieve too much, yet I witnessed Father's great sorrow and was touched by his anguish. As a result of his woes, he turned back to Garth and me for love. There was also, of course, his love child being cared for by Aunt Gwen. These events, the harshness of the war, and his own maturing age meant that his wild oats were now sown. My brother and I at last had a father. Of Mother, on the other side of the world, nothing was known, and it was tactless to ask. She was a taboo subject; on rare occasions she was obliquely referred to as "the scarlet woman who had abandoned her children." Although she always knew how to contact us, she never did.

These were not my only memories of World War II. Back in 1940, the Germans began bombing my hometown, Bristol, a mere fifteen miles from Bath, my birthplace. The justification for these attacks was the city's numerous key industries, including aircraft manufacturing, and an important railroad junction. We slept in a large cupboard under the staircase of Aunt Stella's home. It was supposed to be the structurally safest place in the house and was certainly free from flying glass. With such sturdy stone houses, all but a direct hit meant a person would probably survive under the stairs. At first, the attacks were intended mainly to frighten the population. German engineers put a flange on the wind vane of some of the bombs, causing them to scream as they descended. Whenever one of these special bombs started downwards with its eerie sound, I would call out "Here's a whistle bomb!" and dive for safety under the covers! When the screaming stopped, there was a dull and distant thud. We knew that we were safe but that some others probably had not been so lucky. In the year 1941 alone, German air raids on Britain cost a total of 43,381 civilian lives, with a further 50,856 seriously injured.

As the bombing intensified, the government ordered general evacuation of all children from the cities. Those who could not move in with relatives or friends in the country were gathered together by school authorities and transported in groups to the safety of distant towns and villages. Church halls, schoolrooms, and empty buildings were commandeered by new law. Children were accommodated on camp beds.

During the year 1940, the "committee" of my aunts and uncles debated whether to send Garth and me to the US for safety. We had cousins in Pasadena, California, who were willing to take us. But German submarines were sinking so many ships during the Battle of the Atlantic that it was decided that the risk of sea crossing was greater than staying in England.

So Aunts Gwen and Ena took a bus out to the Mendip Hills, about fifteen miles from Bristol. They tramped the area, knocking on farmhouse doors to ask whether anyone would take two boy evacuees aged twelve and ten. One of the benefits of Father's RAF service was an allowance of fifteen shillings a week for the upkeep of each child. Thus, my brother and I were no longer a financial drain on his siblings. Amazing how far fifteen shillings went in wartime England! Today that sum would only purchase a few newspapers.

This particular upheaval in my life turned out wonderfully well. What followed were the happiest and most formative years of my young life. We were boarded with Ernest and Kate Winter, a sweet couple in their sixties, who ran a one-hundred-acre dairy farm on the Mendip Hills. They had raised six children, but only one, Maurice, remained to help on the farm. With their

family departed, the Winters were happy to have two useful—
and fee-paying—boys to fill the gap. Garth and I were overjoyed
at our new living arrangements and delighted when we were
told we would have to help on the farm. The Winters believed
strongly in the work ethic, but they did not believe in slavery;
duties were carefully apportioned according to physical strength,
and everybody did their bit.

Garth always fetched the cows morning and night at milking
time and brought the horses in from the fields when needed.
The farm was not rich enough to own a tractor; horses were used
for heavy fieldwork. Being smaller, my tasks included feeding the
chickens, collecting the eggs, searching the fields for eggs laid
by roaming broody hens, bringing in the kindling, hunting for
mushrooms, and generally running errands. Garth and I took
turns wiping the dishes as Mrs. Winter washed them. We never
felt that we were overworked because the Winters had such a
pleasant attitude to both domestic and farm life. Instead, it was a
pleasure to be part of a communal effort.

Mr. and Mrs. Winter brought stability, rhythm, the work
ethic, and old-fashioned respect for family values into my life.
Their religious attitude was typical for the time. Mrs. Winter
went to church every Sunday. The grown men did not, but we
boys were ordered to attend Sunday school. No profanity was
ever allowed; within limits you could cuss mildly if you were hurt
or surprised, but not even that was allowed on Sundays. You did
not have to be overtly religious, but you could never take the
Lord's name in vain. The Winters practiced Christian principles
without being too obvious, and I respected that attitude.

England was passing through a strange period in those years.
There were virtually no men and women between the ages
of eighteen and fifty left in civilian life. Britain was fighting a
"total war." Those few who were still at home had "reserved

occupations" of crucial importance. So it was common for children like Garth and me to be raised by the older generations.

For most people, the age period between fifteen and thirty-five is the time of greatest achievement and enjoyment. They carry forward and treasure the impressions and lessons of these years for the remainder of their lives. That important phase in the lives of the Winter couple was somewhere between 1875 and 1905. So their reminiscences were always about the happenings of that period. What I heard talked about a great deal at meal times had mostly taken place fifty years earlier, before the advent of the motorcar, the radio, and the airplane. They would reminisce about going to the seaside, thirty miles away, in a horse and buggy. I grew up in a kind of time warp, something I remain grateful for. There was plenty of time in the rest of my life to enjoy the fruits of modern lifestyle. Years later, when reading Thomas Hardy's novels, particularly *Jude the Obscure* and *Under the Greenwood Tree*, which are set in the nineteenth century, so great was the influence of the Winters' reminiscences that I almost felt that I had lived in that century too.

Because I'd always been a sickly child, prone to chest complaints and every known communicable disease, a great benefit of living on the Winters' farm was the fresh air on the Mendip Hills together with an adequate, if plain, wartime diet. It was part of my duties to help churn the butter and cheese (we had no electricity for gadgets), and the Winters slaughtered their own fowls as well as the occasional pig or calf. With this regimen during my formative years, I grew up healthy and robust and was blessed with good health throughout my youth.

The worst moments of my otherwise idyllic life on the farm were when German bombers in 1941 made their extensive night attacks on Bristol. We were perched on the hills outside of the city, some fifteen miles away, and at times it appeared to be ablaze from end to end. One particular night from the intense glow across the horizon it seemed to me that the entire city must have been destroyed with nearly everybody dead. Next morning, with no bombers within sight or sound, Garth and I cycled off toward Bristol. We promised the fretful Winters that we would not stay the night because it was virtually certain that the air raids would resume after dark. The worst damage was to the city center, where the lovely old buildings and churches went up in flames. Everybody I knew was in surprisingly good physical condition although they were nervous wrecks and extremely short of sleep. The tremendous glow had come from direct hits on the commercial district. Huge blocks of offices, stores, warehouses, and apartments in the city center were gutted by a firestorm.

Hitler boasted on radio that night (so we learned later) that Bristol had been destroyed. It was his usual exaggeration, yet it was a terrible night. Two hundred people were killed in the city and 800 injured. Ten thousand homes were damaged. (Records in the Imperial War Museum.)

I was very relieved that Garth and I had been evacuated. In Knowle, where almost all the family lived, large stores were destroyed. Their sturdy homes had only minor damage to roofs and windows. My old junior school was burned to the ground (every schoolboy's dream!), the imposing, red-brick Holy Nativity Church where the family had worshipped was destroyed, except for its tower. For a time there was no supply of water, gas, or electricity.

In my files recently, I came across the original of a letter that I wrote at the time describing this wartime life. Thanks to circumstances I will shortly explain, I possess the original I wrote on January 10, 1942, to my cousin David Player who lived in Pasadena, California, when I was eleven years old. It was addressed from Vauntpitt Farm, East Harptree, Near Bristol, Somerset, where I was living as an evacuee with the Winter family. It read:

Dear David,

I received your Christmas card on 30th December 1941. I am on a farm on the Mendip Hills by myself for Garth has just gone out to work. I am now 11. My father is an air gunner in the R.A.F. I have two miles to go to school but we have a bus to pick us up. We live in an old farm with a huge fireplace and oven, no electric light or gas, and we make our own butter and sometimes our own bread. My hobby now is building model airplanes from balsa wood. When I grow up I want to be a farmer. I don't know what you want to be. I used to want to be a pilot in the R.A.F. Mr. and Mrs. Winter are the people I am staying with, also a son called Maurice. They have two sons in the army, one abroad, two in the police force, one in the Home Guard, and one daughter. I would like you to write back to me. So cheerio.

Your affectionate cousin, Derek

I have the original envelope addressed by me to "Master D. Player" with a postage stamp showing the head of King George VI on it, costing two-and-a-half pennies. It had been censored. Across the envelope is a label saying "Opened by Examiner 4363." What secrets the censors expected to find in a letter between two eleven-year-old boys are a puzzle, but they were taking no chances. I suppose I could have written to David about the aircraft—British and German—that I had recently witnessed crashing out of the sky, the anti-aircraft guns hidden in nearby woods, and convoys of military constantly passing by. But as I recall, the government's insistence on everybody being cautious about what they said—"Be like Dad, Keep Mum" was the motto on posters everywhere—must have made me keep my news to David confined to the huge fireplace and oven, no electric light, and so on.

How I came to own this letter, sent six thousand miles in 1942, was due to my emigrating to America to join the *Los Angeles Times* in 1978. I went to see my cousins, the Player family in Pasadena, and met with David. But he was not a well man and died shortly after. Following the funeral, his mother gave me this letter and envelope—a surprising flashback into my childhood.

If German submarines had not been sinking so many ships during the Battle of the Atlantic, Garth and I would have been sent to live with the Player family in California. Other less obvious wartime circumstances were to have a profound and long-lasting effect on my life.

The Winters' oldest son, Wesley, had fought in World War I and survived despite the appalling casualties among foot soldiers. The youngest, Cyril, was an army tank driver in this war. Soon after I went to live with the Winters, he was captured in the North African campaign and held prisoner by the Germans. Cyril's well-being became the centerpiece of Mrs. Winter's life. She followed the Allies' misfortunes and then fortunes of war with meticulous detail. As the Allies slowly pushed the Germans back from Africa up through Italy and into Germany from France, Cyril and the thousands of other POWs were moved back, stage by stage, to avoid recapture. If there was Allied progress, Mrs. Winter would speculate where Cyril might be. As she pored over the map, she saw the whole world war through a tunnel vision that focused only on her beloved last-born child. The subtle influence on me came from listening punctiliously with her to the BBC Radio news bulletins at 8 a.m., 1 p.m., and 9 p.m. With no electricity at the farm, the only radio was battery powered, and this had to be conserved. The moment the announcer closed the news bulletin, Mrs. Winter snapped off the power button. If there had been significant news, she would advise us about Cyril's probable new location of captivity.

The consequence of these thrice-daily news briefings by the BBC over four years, with the exclusion of all else, was the development of my lifelong interest in world current affairs. When Mrs. Winter was out of the house, I would sometimes listen to Alistair Cooke's *Letter from America* on the BBC. His gift of expression and succinctness impressed me greatly. As a result, I decided at the age of thirteen to become a journalist with the eventual aim of becoming an author. The world of communication was where I belonged. Working on a farm, in an office, or with my hands, was never even considered. I was determined to be a writer.

The other curious effect of the war was that I had very little formal education. Even before the war, because of the constant family troubles, my schooling was sketchy; now it was pretty well nonexistent. Country schools were grossly overcrowded with children sent out from the cities. Teachers under fifty were drafted for the war effort, so a few old people came out of retirement to try to help. At Priddy School, there were about a hundred children between the ages of five and fourteen cared for by two elderly teachers. Many times children were sent home because there was nowhere to sit. There was prim Miss Mullett, who struggled with the infants, and the elderly headmistress Lucy Reeves, who fought with the others. We were a boisterous, unruly lot, more interested in the state of the war and working on the farms than education, which we considered unnecessary. But Miss Reeves handled us shrewdly, at least in my case. With so many pupils in so wide an age range there was little chance for formal classroom lessons. Miss Reeves broke the scholars up into little groups and gave them projects. She soon singled me out as a potential bookworm. Whenever I walked through the door she would usually thrust a book into my hands and command, "Go over there Derek and read this." It was just what I relished: self-education. As I was later to realize, this freedom to learn was not good enough. In that period, and for many years after, English schoolchildren took what was called the "eleven-plus exam," the results of which decided their educational path. My brother and all my cousins passed the examination and won scholarships to good schools. It was my bad luck to be eleven years old in 1941, the height of the war, and in the prevailing educational chaos, nobody offered me the examination.

By this stage of the war, as Germany pressed home its sinister naval blockade, the shortage of labor on the farms was so acute and the need for food so desperate that it was decided to use schoolchildren as field-workers where possible. So it became a routine of school—such as it was—in the mornings, and then after lunch we were given a green card with a farmer's name and address on it. We would tramp there to pick fruit, gather potatoes, pull turnips, or do other light work. Nothing too heavy was required of us, just the use of our supple bodies and nimble fingers. We all preferred this to the boring, overcrowded school and being bossed about by old ladies. For their part, the stressed-out education authorities in the rural areas got a welcome relief from overcrowding.

My cup ran over: books in the morning, light farmwork in the afternoon, and the nourishing warmth of the Winter family in the evening and at weekends. They were such real people—calm, caring, and tolerant—they became my role models. It was my great good fortune to have what is sometimes paradoxically known as a "good war."

* * *

As the war gradually turned in the Allies' favor, the Mendip Hills, indeed most of Somerset (now renamed Avon) was declared an "exclusion zone" in preparation for D-Day, the Normandy landing. No visitors or travelers were allowed. The country roads were packed with parked trucks, jeeps, armored cars, light artillery, and tanks. It was a boy's dreamworld. The soldiers with all this equipment were not allowed to leave it for any purpose. So we kids struck up deals. The soldiers would beg us to go and buy cigarettes for them. We agreed to do so as long as they let us get up on their tank and look in. My favorite bribe was agreeing to do their shopping provided I could first get up on the seat of a howitzer—light gun—and twirl the wheels so as to swivel around and pretend to aim it at a nearby hill. Totally against the rules, but we did it only when the officers were not looking.

The only aspect of farm life that I hated was the prevalence of poisonous snakes. Huge areas of the Mendips were wild and too rocky and undulating to cultivate, a perfect haven for reptiles. Adders (also known as vipers) were abundant. They have a bite that can make a person very ill, though rarely fatally. In wartime Britain, gas was rationed. There weren't many motorcars anyway, and buses were few and far between. And a lively boy like me did not have the patience to take the long routes along the roads. I traveled fast across country, developing a series of shortcuts across fields and woods that reduced journeys by many miles. On weekdays, a school bus picked us up, but going to Sunday School or seeking a playmate at a nearby farm would entail trotting for miles across country. Yet trekking through this rough country in summertime risked meeting snakes galore. I learned to walk with my eyes fixed about fifteen feet ahead. If an adder reared up ahead when my footsteps surprised it, there was time to stop and let it slither away. Snakes don't want to bite you except in self-defense. The most often bitten were small children running pell-mell, bare-legged through long grass, and stepping on frightened snakes.

But one snake experience left me shattered at the time and implanted an enduring phobia about reptiles. On a hot summer's day, one of my rapid cross-country trips took me through a familiar hole in a thorn fence. As I passed out of the shadows into the fierce sunlight on the other side, before I could do anything about it, I found I had crawled on top of an adder, about four feet long. The snake looked at me and I stared at it—I don't know which of us was the more frightened! Much of its body was pinned beneath me, and its face was a few inches from mine. I was physically unable to move upwards because of the low aperture in the fence. Nor could I go forward or backwards without concentrating my weight on the snake.

In what seemed like hours but was in reality seconds, the snake managed to wiggle away without hurting me. But the shock was so great that I burst from the hole and took off like an Olympic sprinter. After a few hundred yards, I collapsed in a paroxysm of tears of relief for my escape. Perhaps the snake was doing the same! Again, I know that snakes do not bite humans if they can help it, and it is unreasonable of me to fear them as much as I do. But we all have our little phobias, and mine is concerned with reptiles. I suppose it has something to do with the mystery and the pain of receiving a lightning-quick poisonous bite that might kill you. Anyway, for the rest of my stay at the farm, every night before getting into bed, I stripped away all the bedclothes to ensure that there were no snakes present between the sheets. The impossibility of a snake getting into the farmhouse and up the stairs and into my bed was something I refused to acknowledge.

The happiest times in the country were, of course, harvesting and haymaking. Ours was a small farm, surrounded by other equally small spreads, so they were run like a cooperative. We shared the heavy equipment and all pitched in when the crops needed gathering quickly. Being small, I was the messenger and errand boy for urgent necessities. Mostly this involved running back to the farmhouse for the cider and bread and cheese at break times. My reward was to mix with the hearty men as they sat in the fields, eating and gossiping.

Sometimes we heard aircraft overhead and would look up to see combat between the RAF and the Luftwaffe going on in the sky. The German fighters were unable to get as far as Somerset, leaving the bombers with no protection. Whenever an aircraft was crippled and started to crash land I'd watch the trajectory and try to guess where it would fall. Then I'd mount my bicycle and pedal furiously in that direction. Mostly I misjudged, giving up many miles from the actual landing spot, but on one occasion I got it right and had the dreamlike, schoolboy joy of sitting in the pilot's seat of a Heinkel bomber. This happened only an hour after the pilot, who had taken off that morning from a German base in France, had vacated it. Soon, other boys joined me and we "manned" this aircraft for hours until the army engineers arrived to cart it away, but not before we had collected lots of souvenirs. The Humphry family had no military service tradition and would have preferred not to be in the armed services. But Britain was fighting a total war, thus Father was in RAF aircrew, Uncle Leonard was a prisoner of war, Uncle Horace was an RAF mechanic, cousin Rodney Brimble, a fighter pilot, was shot down in the Battle of Britain, and brother Garth enlisted at seventeen for the last six months of the war. Uncle Wilfred was exempt because he was a skilled draftsman working on portable military bridges and the pontoon harbor for D-Day. But most nights he was on duty as an air raid warden, one of the thousands of people who rushed around during an air raid putting buckets of sand on incendiary bombs before they took hold.

As the months and the war dragged on, I began to sense that before long I would have to earn my living someday. Two things troubled me. I had heard and read about the Great Depression of the 1930s, and it seemed logical to me that, given the cost of the war and the damage done, an economic condition like that would resume after hostilities ended. Secondly, there were constant reminders that hundreds of thousands of service men and women would be returning to civilian life at the war's conclusion. Jobs would have to be found for them. I cursed my bad luck at the prospect of being an entrant to the job market at such an unpropitious time. Oddly enough, because of Sybil's death and a lesser war pressure on him, it was then that Father was taking a greater interest in my well-being, particularly the gaping hole in my education. He realized just how poor my formal schooling was. I was almost entirely lacking in mathematics, grammar, history, and geography. True, I was extraordinarily well read, but this literary asset was not readily appreciated by employers. Father insisted that it was time to leave the farm and attend a better school in Bristol. As much as I hated the idea of such a separation, I knew he was right, and in tears, I agreed. The happiest time of my boyhood was over.

But remember, I had ambitions to be a writer, and even at thirteen, common sense told me that I needed more education to even begin to achieve this. I moved back to Bristol, no longer being bombed as the war went the way of the Allies, to live with Aunt Stella and try a fresh school. It did not work out well. To begin with, I was so far behind academically, and the teachers recruited from Ireland had such strong brogue accents, that I could not understand most of what they said. So when I was ready to leave school at the legally permitted age of fifteen, my education was extremely slender. All I could claim was that I was literate. I guessed I could build on that! There was no choice.

Around the age of fourteen, I developed a passion for listening to classical music. It has ever since been an inspiration, pleasure, and support all my life. I work, drive, and relax with concert music playing in the background the same way so many young people today spend their time listening to pop and rock. At the same time, I don't understand the technical aspects of music and I've never played a musical instrument.

My love of classical music came to me through voices of two women. Close to home, Aunt Gwen had a glorious contralto voice and was in constant demand to sing in area concerts and oratorios. She was never quite good enough to be a professional but she was a top-class amateur. Listening casually to her practicing at home, singing to her own piano accompaniment, strongly influenced my taste in music. Additionally, in 1944 a famous soprano singer, Isobel Baillie, had a fifteen-minute program on the BBC Radio that was broadcast right after I returned home from school. I was her most devoted fan. Her glorious renditions of the world's great songs sent this fourteen-year-old into raptures. From there to the concertos of Beethoven, Bach, and Mozart was an easy transition.

Chapter 2

RUNAWAY

THE CATALYST FOR MY decision to leave this hodgepodge of a family at fifteen was a religious dispute. My aunts and uncles were steady churchgoers in the Protestant faith—high Church of England, in fact. They assumed without asking that I shared their beliefs. However, because I had so much spare school time on my hands, my reading had included such radicals as Bernard Shaw, H. G. Wells, and Thomas Paine—unbelievers all. I was deeply impressed by Wells's *An Outline of History*. I concluded that if his version of the world's beginning was anywhere near right, then there was no room for the Christian six-day version of the creation in my personal beliefs. Then I read the works of Charles Darwin, and that clinched my atheism. I was impressed, too, by Shaw's theory of a "life force." I took that to mean that there was in everyone the will to live to the fullest extent of their ability while at the same time being considerate of others. While respecting that others might feel differently, deep down I just did not feel any faith in a supernatural being nor in any form of afterlife.

So when the aunts fixed a date for my combined baptism (it had been overlooked when I was a baby in the chaos of my parents' failing marriage) and confirmation as a member of the Church of England, I rebelled. My protestations that I was not spiritually ready for these ceremonies fell on deaf ears. That served only to underline my suspicion that much religion is an automatic response to social and familial pressures. I decided it was time to leave the family and tackle the world by myself.

On April 29, 1945, my fifteenth birthday arrived, so I could legally quit school. In anticipation, for the prior few months I had been begging local newspaper editors to employ me as a cub reporter, but I was turned down regularly. The reason given was that employers were legally obliged to reemploy, when the end of the war came, all those men who had worked for them in the past six years. It was a depressing time to be joining the world of work.

I decided to clear out on the Sunday of my intended baptism and confirmation. My plan was to get to London and join a newspaper. I had ten shillings of my own, and my brother loaned me another ten, enough for a one-way train fare from Bristol to London. Because the war in Europe was almost finished, Father had obtained an early release from the air force. They had taken into account his joining up before the war, his war wounds, and his excellent record. I knew that he was living somewhere in West London, probably Ealing, so after getting off the train I made straight for that district. Of course, I didn't find him straight off. Completely broke, I nevertheless persuaded the kindly owners of a boarding house to put me up for one week. The rent was one pound, ten shillings.

"I'll have a job on a newspaper in a couple of days and then I'll be able to pay you," I optimistically told the owners. Either they believed me or they took pity on this cocky, pimply youth from the provinces, I never knew which. Anyway, I had a bed for a few nights.

The next morning was Monday and I took the bus into central London, heading for the newspaper district, Fleet Street, which is (or was) also known as "the street of adventure." I walked slowly up and down and stared at the giant, forbidding newspaper buildings, pondering how to make my assault. At the *Daily Telegraph* and the *Daily Express* I ventured into the plate glass front offices where I was immediately confronted by large, ex-military men dressed in the uniforms of the London Corps of Commissionaires. When I told them I was looking for work as a reporter, they said, "Write a letter of application," and gently ushered me out of their palaces.

Strolling further down Fleet Street, I realized that this door-stepping approach to journalism was not likely to get me far. I was stranded. At the bottom of the street, in Ludgate Circus, there was a new government employment bureau. Thinking I might get some advice here, I strolled in. The place was empty— they were preparing for the crowd of military demobilized job seekers due any time now—and they seemed quite glad to see me. I told the man at the desk that I needed a job as a journalist and waited while he thumbed through a large Rolodex file. My spirits rose when he said that the London office of the *Yorkshire Post* needed an "editorial assistant." This was a newspaper that I had never seen but knew it was a significant North Country provincial journal.

"That sounds just like me," I said eagerly. The clerk made a telephone call and made an appointment for me to see the *Post*'s London editor at noon that very day. I thanked the employment clerk profusely and walked out into the sunshine on top of the world. I was on my way into journalism, starting quite close to the top! During the interview the editor, A. E. Holdsworth, said that the wage would be two pounds a week. I silently calculated that after paying for my room, this would leave me just ten shillings for travel and meals. Not much, but just enough to get by on.

Though Mr. Holdsworth explained that the working hours would be 5 p.m. until midnight, he said very little about what the job entailed. I was too ignorant and too excited to ask about that.

"When can you start?"

He was a little surprised when I responded, "Tonight, sir." He signed me up, and I left, walking on air for the whole afternoon, just waiting for 5 p.m. and the start of my first job. What would they think at home and at my old school when they heard that I had landed a job on a newspaper, in Fleet Street no less?

My feet touched the ground a few minutes after 5 p.m. when I reported for duty. Tom Loveless, the grizzled, white-haired chief subeditor informed me that my first assignment was to hunt for a packet of cigarettes! I ran from pub bar to cafe to kiosk, but in wartime Britain there were none to be had. I wondered why he had even sent me on this fruitless mission.

Trying to mollify Mr. Loveless, I told him: "They all say they'll have some tomorrow." Not being a smoker, I did not realize that his need was for the here and now, not another day. Grumpily, he accepted my explanation.

"Now take this to the news editor of the *Daily Telegraph*," he ordered. It was a dispatch from a war correspondent. In those difficult days, newspapers were obliged to share correspondents based in the different theaters of war. Returning from the *Telegraph*, I was told to get my boss a cup of tea and a sandwich. Then off with an article to the Ministry of Information so that it could be censored. By the end of the evening, I knew that "editorial assistant" was a euphemism for messenger boy. I was not going to be asked to write anything. Yet I had my foot in the door. I was getting survival wages, and this was certainly better than nothing.

The job entailed a lot of hanging around the editorial office of the *Post* and other newspapers, waiting for errands. I made good use of this situation by becoming an observer. I soaked up newspaper atmosphere and parlance and learned a lot of new cuss words of a type they didn't use down on the farm. Soon I began to think and act like a newspaperman, although I still hadn't written a single word. After a few weeks, I got a break that began my career as a journalist.

Mr. Holdsworth was not getting enough material to fill his "Letter from London," which appeared in the northern newspaper every day. This column consisted of five or six gossipy stories, each approximately five paragraphs long, about things that happened in the nation's capital that day. Mr. Holdsworth organized the stories, and Mr. Loveless did the copyediting. Gradually they began to give me small assignments for the next day with instructions to arrive for my normal 5 p.m. work shift with the copy already written. These assignments were usually about the opening of an exhibition, the preview of a new movie, or a press conference. The war was ending, and these were heady times in London. The wraps came off hundreds of secrets, and creative people sought to make their mark again. For instance, it seems silly to report this now, but I was one of the first civilians ever to see frogmen. Before the war there had been no such thing as frogmen, with wet suits, flippers, and breathing equipment. Their development during the war was a tight secret from the civilian population, but not, I suspect, from the Germans. I had the honor of reporting from a swimming pool in central London the first civilian view of marine commandos acting as human underwater fishes.

Victory in Europe Day took place on May 8, 1945. Hanging out of the windows of the newspaper office, I watched thousands of men and women dancing in the street, celebrating wildly the end of six long, hard years of hostilities with the Germans. I did not feel like joining the mass dancing but I felt a profound sense of relief. There was still concern about how Japan was going to be tackled. Everyone dreaded that awful remaining part of the war. Of course, we knew nothing about the atomic bomb that answered that question a few months later. I was finding it hard to live in London on a mere ten shillings a week. I kept dropping hints to my two bosses that I would most appreciate those assignments that included any form of food. The lofty Mr. Holdsworth ignored my need, but the kindly, if gruff, Mr. Loveless did his best. In 1945 we were great friends with the Russians, our victorious allies, so I went to lots of previews of Russian films. Some were magnificent, but most were very boring. Along with the movie went pretty girls handing out caviar and canapés during the showing. This was made to order for a hungry youth!

At fifteen, with my appalling lack of formal education and sophistication, I was a terrible writer. But Mr. Loveless was determined to knock some basic skills into me. As I have said, each story was only five or six paragraphs long. That may sound easy, but conciseness and compression of a big issue are an art— one which I completely lacked. A typical evening's work for me was rushing to the office by 4 p.m. That allowed me an hour to type up my story for the 5 p.m. deadline.

An hour later Mr. Loveless would boom: "Humphry!"

"Yes, sir!"

"This is terrible." He'd explain why. "Do it again." I was unable to write in the main newsroom because I was constantly asked to fetch cigarettes and cups of tea. Right at the top of the rickety Victorian building I found the office of somebody who was never there. Above the fray, I pounded out rewrite after rewrite on an old Remington typewriter. It was not unusual for my two bosses to ask me to rewrite my contribution four or five times every evening. But I was happy to be a writer at last, even if the final printed version bore only the slightest resemblance to my original. The discipline of careful thought and simple brevity pounded into me by those veteran journalists served me well for the rest of my life. That year I spent most mornings reading books by George Bernard Shaw, particularly his *Everybody's Political What's What*, which had just been published. Religiously, I checked the dictionary for each word I didn't understand perfectly. I appreciated little of the great playwright's political theories, but his command of the English language was towering. From this experience, I began to develop a vocabulary and I longed to use it. I wrote poems and essays and sent a few to magazines. Naturally, they all came whistling back with rejection notices. I didn't mind. That—or so I had read—was routine treatment for all beginning writers. And again and again, I started to write novels, but at this age my ideas were so poorly formed, my life experience so thin, that they never got beyond the first couple of chapters. One free afternoon I spent in the House of Commons, and that evening I wrote what is called "a parliamentary sketch" of about a thousand words. The next morning, I confidently delivered it by hand to the offices of one of the leading political journals in the country, the *New Statesman and Nation*. It was rejected. Looking back, I marvel at my effrontery and naiveté in thinking that such an intellectual journal would accept a political article from a callow youth. But I was willing to stop at nothing to make my mark. Rejection slips may be harsh, but at least you don't hear the editor's scornful laughter!

After six weeks, I telephoned Aunt Gwen and told her that I was happily settled in London, working for a newspaper (without detailing my status on it) and not to worry about me. I announced that I intended to look after myself for the rest of my life. Eventually, I tracked down my father and got some vicarious pleasure in seeing his amazed countenance when I described what I was doing. We got on well and a few weeks later began to share a small room in Holland Park. It was closer to central London and meant—given that I usually had all day free—I could walk to work and save the travel fares. I had only just enough money for one hot meal a day, with perhaps a snack in the evening. Father was secretive about his situation but it seemed to me that he was out of work. He needed me even more than I needed him. One day I had no money for food and walked around bookstores most of the day trying to sell my books by Shaw. No one would pay anything for them, so, hungry and angry, I threw them in the River Thames and reported for work. For me—the dreaming, future literary lion—to throw four books by my favorite author into a river was strange conduct indeed. I must have been extremely frustrated. Luckily, one of the paper's other messenger boys had some money. He generously bought me a cheese-on-toast snack at the *Daily Express* canteen, and I made it through the night.

When my salary was raised to two pounds and ten shillings after six months, I was able, if I was frugal, to save enough to visit an occasional cinema or symphony concert. I longed to go to the opera, the ballet, and the theater—art forms that were blossoming in postwar London—but it was financially impossible. So I haunted the National Gallery and the Tate Gallery, killing time sitting and looking at the paintings and sculptures and occasionally hearing the celebrated free lunchtime piano concerts of Dame Myra Hess. For variety, I spent hours in the rambling bookstores in the Charing Cross Road area without ever buying a book. I did not suffer from loneliness or boredom because I was afloat in the world of art and literature that I revered. Being a "culture vulture" saved my sanity and contributed enormously to my improving education.

After Father and I started living together, I had a small amount of money to spare. I was able to visit a theater in the Haymarket to see a matinee performance of Oscar Wilde's *The Importance of Being Earnest* and observe the great actress Edith Evans give her famous slow, throaty delivery of two words: "A handbag!" As I recollect, I paid two shillings and sixpence to sit in the "Gods"—as the top tier balcony was called, because of its proximity to heaven. Once, I was able to afford attending a Promenade Concert in the Albert Hall to hear Thomas Beacham conduct some magnificent Beethoven.

I did not avoid formal education altogether. Realizing that I could not be a good reporter without being able to write shorthand—this was before the days of tape recorders—I attended classes several days a week at the Pitman Shorthand College in Russell Square. I struggled to become proficient in this form of speedwriting, but I never did. My handwriting was just a large scrawl; speedwriting medium requires a small, neat hand. Over the following years I became competent enough to take brief notes in shorthand but I was never able to take a speech verbatim, as some of my colleagues could.

Father was always chasing women, including a well-known music-hall singer named Maudie Edwards. Sometimes I went with him on a Saturday to one of her performances. The coarseness of the language she and her fellow artistes used shocked this puritanical, provincial boy, a "culture vulture" who loved the loftier arts. I noticed, however, that the rest of the audience adored the smutty language. Afterwards, Ms. Edwards, or somebody else

in her retinue, usually bought me a good dinner, so I was wise
enough to keep my moral reservations to myself. They would
have considered me a cultural snob, which I suppose I was.

Thus my sixteenth year, spent in what could fairly be described
as a "new London," was a crash course in self-education, artistic
appreciation, rudimentary political knowledge, and the elements
of journalism. It all came to an end suddenly when Father said
that we must leave London immediately. He would not tell me
why, hinting only that it was woman trouble. I believed this at
the time but later realized that it was business trouble. Not that
I was unaware of Father's blemishes—the rest of the family had
drummed into me for years that he was a liar and a cheat and
was totally unreliable. I personally knew him to be a thief since
he had pocketed five pounds that had been given to him to hand
over to me. So I knew that I was dealing with a father who was
shifty. But he was a loveable rogue. We were both at the bottom
of the heap, struggling to exist, and we needed each other. When
he begged me to flee from London with him I told him it would
ruin my fledgling journalistic career. But using that persuasive
charm that was his only asset, Father said that he had a journalist
friend in Bristol, Jimmy James, who would secure me a job on a
newspaper. We hastily packed our few belongings and returned
to Bristol by train. I had been away a full year.

For once Father had spoken the truth. Mr. James arranged
an interview for me with Reginald Eason, the news editor of the
Evening World. When I related to Mr. Eason the story of my year
in London, he seemed impressed and offered me a job as cub
reporter at three pounds a week. Father and I took a one-room
apartment room in Clifton, and I prepared for stage two of my
career.

How Father existed was a mystery. Always scrupulously
dressed in a black pinstripe suit, white handkerchief neatly

folded in top pocket, clean white shirt (even if the cuffs could be seen on close examination to be frayed), he was the epitome of the smart businessman. Beautifully mannered, well spoken, a knockout with the women, why, I wondered, was he so poor? An inordinately proud man, he would confide to me nothing of what was really going on in his life. "Something really big will turn up," he used to say, just like Dickens's Mr. Micawber.

Despite his magnificent front, I knew something was terribly wrong when he began taking money from me in the most pathetic way. We lived, as I said, in one room, and he would rise early, shave, dress, and be ready to leave long before I was up. Often, I would actually be awake, but, reluctant to get up, I'd remain as though asleep. Then he would creep across the room to where my small change had been left on a mantle shelf when I'd undressed. He would sort through the cash and take several shillings, just enough to buy himself a meal during the day. I felt so sad about his desperate state that I never reproached him and always feigned sleep. I gradually realized that he was one of the thousands of dejected, unemployed men who spent their days in library reading rooms. He was too proud to let me know. I was unaware of a deeper problem. After a while, his habit of taking some of my money stopped, and he looked a little more prosperous. I assumed that he had found work. I myself was wonderfully happy. My job as a junior reporter involved helping the news editor get the evening paper tasks assigned. I typed the list of the day's news events in which all the reporters' tasks were detailed. Mine, of course, were the most mundane: the weather, road accidents, fire and ambulance calls. In the 1940s, there were relatively few automobiles. Local newspapers reported traffic accidents even if they did not involve human injury. I visited the scene and wrote up many a "fender bender." Another common assignment was reporting the countless grease fires that took

place in fish and chip shops. As I would be scooting enthusiastically out of the newsroom, the older reporters would good-
humoredly mock, "Humphry's chasing another frying pan fire!"
It was all right for them, writing the serious stuff, but I had to
earn a living too.

Sometimes, as part of my training, I would sit in the courts
with an experienced reporter, watch him at work, read his copy,
and take it back to the office. Then the daily news assignments
began to put my name against "Divorce Courts." This sort of
reporting taught me nothing about journalism but a lot about
married life. The law in England at that time permitted uncon-
tested divorce proceedings to be reported, yet restricted to just
the names of the parties, their addresses, and the judge's reason for the dissolution. But to acquire these basic facts I had to
sit through the entire hearing. None of the evidence could be
reported, but the stories that emerged of adult marital behavior
opened the eyes of a sixteen-year-old. I heard about the most
curious sexual behavior that even today would be unreport-
able. Mostly, however, the cases turned on a wife who was left
stranded for five or six years by a husband serving overseas in the
armed services, or one who was a prisoner of war, and the resulting burden of loneliness. Or men and women who had married
hurriedly in their late teens as the man was "shipping out." I
developed no illusions about the simplicity of married bliss from
this daily divorce court experience.

Chapter 3

GETTING TO THE TRUTH

OVER THE NEXT FORTY years, I attended many murder trials in Britain and America. None was more unusual and sensational than the very first trial I listened to in my seventeenth year. I was still a cub reporter at the time, assigned to sit with the senior reporters at Bristol Assizes (the English name for courts that try serious crimes). My job was to help them by running messages and to take their handwritten copy back to the news desk. This murder trial was by far the most famous of the century in Bristol. It even went into the national records in books about homicides.

In the dock, accused of murdering her husband, was a young woman, Mrs. Rosina Cornock. An attractive woman accused of murder is always a sensation, but this one was pregnant and alleged to have as a lover a crippled man who lodged in her house. Cecil George Cornock had been found drowned in his bath under suspicious circumstances. He was perfectly healthy but had multiple injuries to his head and limbs. Marks on his wrists and ankles showed that he had been recently bound by cords. Moreover, letters described as "affectionate" that had passed between Mrs. Cornock and the crippled lodger were found by the police. Further damning Mrs. Cornock was evidence that two hours had elapsed between her finding her husband submerged in the bath and calling for help. The prosecution claimed that she had tied her husband to the bath with cords, stunned him with their ten-year-old son's toy boat, and then held him under the water. The cause of death was drowning, not any of the blows.

As if a divorce court education in the vagaries of marital life weren't enough, then it was revealed to all in court that Mr. Cornock was a sexual pervert who specialized in bondage. He enjoyed the physical pain inflicted on him by others. His specialty was in being beaten while tied to the tripod of an electric boiler. The defense said the cord marks on his flesh were made by Mr. Cornock during such bondage, and they called scientific experts to say that the nature of the head injuries were too slight to have been inflicted by the large wooden boat that weighed a pound and a half. They asserted that the head injuries were received as Mrs. Cornock and the lodger tried to pull the six-foot-tall man from the bath. They had half-carried, half-dragged him from the bathroom to a bedroom and tried to revive him with artificial respiration.

What was the truth? Both prosecution and defense stories seemed believable. A decision turned on the extent of the injuries to the dead man's head. The prosecution said that the posthumous photographs showed them to be extremely serious. But the famous criminal pathologist Bernard Spilsbury examined the photographs and, drawing on some fifty years of experience, asked one simple question: "What form of photography had been used by the police?" It turned out that the orthochromatic plates used to photograph the dead man's head made the color red appear black. Thus the apparent bruises were in fact slight abrasions caused without the use of violence. So, the story of minor injuries occurring as Mr. Cornock was pulled from the bath became the more credible.

I remember the high drama of the jury's return from its deliberations. Don't forget, in 1947 England, Mrs. Cornock could have been hanged within six weeks if found guilty and her appeal dismissed. To my great joy, because I felt great sympathy for her, the jury reached a verdict of not guilty, and she disappeared into private life to have her baby. Whether she ever married the lodger I do not know. In those days, newspapers allowed people to go quietly back to their own lives.

The other murder trials I observed and helped report usually involved straightforward domestic violence or were the result of drunken fights. I also reported scores of cases of minor criminal behavior. It was not uncommon for the convicted person to approach me—or any other reporter—after the hearing and beg for their case to be omitted from the newspaper, pleading that the shame of publicity would ruin them. Some threatened suicide if we published. So far as I know, none ever did kill themselves. Occasionally people would offer me considerable sums of money to tear up my story. When I refused, they would stuff the money in my pocket. I always removed and returned it. This was an unpleasant aspect of journalism, but if you agree to leave some cases out then you are vulnerable to all requests. It seemed to me that for many, the shame of publication was greater punishment than the actual court conviction.

Interspersed with these few unpleasant assignments were plenty of commissions to report flower shows, plays put on by amateur dramatic societies, or sporting events. I reported on everything from hockey to boxing to soccer. Whether you knew anything about the subject or the sport was irrelevant—what you did not know you had to find out. The first rule of reporting was "Never show your ignorance!" I survived by reporting facts only and avoiding all comment. Between courts and the community, I reported a rich panoply of urban life, all of which made for a broadening career experience. There is, however, a double-edged sword to reporting news events, as I was soon to learn.

The Revelation

By the time I had been a cub reporter for two years, I was accepted as one of the *Evening World*'s regular reporters, part of a team that was producing top-flight journalism. I was an avid participant in the teasing and sharp-witted camaraderie that was particularly evident back when journalists all sat around one large table. Today, reporters have individual desks from which to operate their computers, and the camaraderie is gone. At nearly eighteen, I was firmly established on the first rung of the ladder to a successful career in journalism. Evening newspapers in a time before television printed about six or eight editions every day as they sought to be the first paper to print not only the news but also sports results. The main edition, in which the cream of the day's news was gathered in a polished manner, came out at 2:30 p.m. Afterward, it was the custom of the journalists to have a sort of "quiet period" while the quality of the day's work was assessed.

On January 14, 1948, during that reflective period, I was at the big table with about fifteen senior reporters, when I opened my paper to the center page spread. My blood ran cold at the following story:

AFTER ACQUITTAL BRISTOL PUBLISHER
COLLAPSES IN COURT

Leaving the dock after he had been acquitted at Exeter
yesterday of four charges of obtaining money by false
pretences, Alfred Royston Humphry, 44, publisher, of 29
Whiteladies Road, Bristol, staggered and fell into a seat.
He was revived with smelling salts.

Humphry was charged with obtaining four pounds
and ten shillings for advertisements from four people
in Exeter by the false pretence that he was a representa-
tive of Classified Business and Professional Directory of
Lakeside Road, London W 14.

He pleaded not guilty, denied he claimed money as
being owed, and said a Bristol printer had set in type parts
of two directories he was publishing. Herbert Walter
Logan, printer, of Weir Street, Bristol, produced proofs
and covers of the directories.

Mr. C. F. Ingle, who defended, said the only real criticism that could be made of the business was that it had
no permanent address.

With dread and shame, I looked around the room to see if any
of my colleagues were reading the same story. What were they
thinking? Any second I expected to be asked, "Is this your father
on page four, Derek?" My shock was not just from the publicity—that would be hypocritical for a journalist—but at being
associated with criminal behavior that involved publishing and
honesty. A journalist without integrity was unemployable. The
silence in the newsroom continued to a point where I could bear
it no longer. I went for a walk outside the office. Returning after
a while, nothing was said. The incident was never mentioned by

my colleagues. Whether this was because they did not connect the names or because they were too decent to embarrass me, I shall never know. Considering that these people were astute journalists, accustomed to assessing facts, I suspect that it was out of decency, for which I am grateful to them. Despite all my previous ups and downs in life, this shock was by far the worst, magnified by the fact that the information was right in front of a bunch of colleagues at the newsroom table.

When I had gone for that breather, I'd purchased the rival newspaper, the *Evening Post*. It carried much the same story, with the addition of a final paragraph that showed that Father's escape was a near thing: the Bench decided that there was an element of doubt, of which the accused was given the benefit.

I went to see Aunt Gwen and asked her if she had seen the news. Not only did she say that she had but she informed me that it was not the first time Father had been in trouble. She explained that before the war, he had sold advertisements that were never published and had gone to prison for this scam. Perhaps, she said, the police pounced again because of his record. Then the light went on in my mind: that was why he had disappeared for so long when I was a child, why he volunteered to be a tail gunner in the war, and why he couldn't get work when peace came. In those days, puritanical and harshly judgmental values prevailed. Being an ex-jailbird was a tough stigma to live down. I felt no anger toward him, only immense sadness at his weakness and the trouble it caused him.

The next day I tried to talk to him about the court case, but he was so embarrassed he would not open up to me. "It was all a mistake," he muttered. "It should never have happened." Twenty years later, I again gently broached the subject of the prison sentence, using the excuse that I wanted to understand my own childhood better. Again, he was tremendously embarrassed and defensive. All

I got was, "If so-and-so had sent the check I would not have been convicted." It was typical of Father to blame everyone but himself. He probably started out meaning to publish the advertisements when he took the order. But he was so badly organized in his business and private life, he yielded to temptation and kept the money, convincing himself that he would publish later on.

Despite my busy work life, I was a somewhat lonely youth. I had none of the customary family ties or school connections to the community in which I lived, and there was little chance of meeting young people of my own age. Even more isolating, I was so absorbed in classical music, opera, ballet, theater, books, and poetry—subjects that my contemporaries seemed to care little or nothing about. Another reason was that my work as a reporter kept me busy many evenings and always on Saturdays, when most social events or organized sports took place.

The one person who noticed my loneliness was Mervyn. A tall, powerfully built man about thirty years old, always dressed in a smart, double-breasted pinstripe suit, he ran the mail room at the *Evening World*. His appearance was more appropriate to a successful city businessman than the guy who sorted the letters and parcels and delivered them by hand around the building. Mervyn would often draw me aside into conversation in a pleasant manner. I soon realized that he was different, but I could not quite assess why. Today, homosexual behavior is widely talked about and accepted by many, but in the 1940s it was a strictly taboo subject. At sixteen, I knew nothing about it. I had vaguely heard of some people being referred to as "queers" but did not comprehend the meaning. Several times Mervyn and I went to the theater and concerts together, for he was a most agreeable and intelligent companion. At last I had a friend who could talk about the arts that I loved. On that basis, our friendship would have been fine, but one evening Mervyn invited me to his apartment for supper and afterwards tried to kiss me. He was very gentle and considerate in his wooing, but I was not at all responsive. Romance at any level with another man did not appeal to me. To his credit, he did not push himself on me, and although our friendship cooled somewhat, we remained on speaking terms. A few days later, Father approached me in a panic. He said that friends had told him that I was going around with "the most notorious queer in Bristol." By then, I was able to tell him firmly that I knew what I was doing and that I was not like Mervyn anyway.

To the contrary, my eyes were fixed on a pretty girl who worked in the central city library. I assumed that because she worked in a library she must share my literary interests. But I was so shy and clumsy that I did not dare or even know how to approach her. I was so unsophisticated then that I had the silly notion that a boy somehow declared his love for a girl immediately when they met. I was writing a lot of poetry at the time, so I composed a sonnet declaring my love and brought it to the library during my lunch hour. It took some time for me to build up the courage, but I finally slid the poem across the top of a filing cabinet where she was standing and working. Then I hastily beat a retreat to the back of the library, intending to watch the results. Instead, I panicked and fled out of the door and never returned. In retrospect, I realized how stupid my actions were and how they must have greatly puzzled the young woman. Obviously I had read too many French novels!

After World War II, balls and banquets were popular in social circles. There was the Police Ball, the Symphony Orchestra Ball, the Press Ball, and so forth. To me, this seemed to be the epitome of bright society. But I could not dance and I did not have a girl to take to the ball. To solve this problem I enrolled in ballroom dancing classes. How embarrassed I was to find that the only pupils at the dance school were I and another young woman. So we received private instruction. Though I never became much of a dancer, I learned enough to get by in the waltz and the quickstep. Tangos, fox-trots, and the like defeated me. My dancing partner was a pleasant woman about my age. We became friendly, and I invited her to have lunch with me one day. With the passage of time I have forgotten her name, but I remember what a mess I also made of this encounter. Once again I overdid it. She accepted my invitation to go to London by train, look around, and have lunch. I took her to the only restaurant in London whose name was familiar to me: the Cafe Royal. I had frequently read that it was the famous literary haunt of Max Beerbohm, Oscar Wilde, Bernard Shaw, H. G. Wells, and others. I did not realize how grand it was until we were seated. Then came another shock: the waiters spoke only French, although ours was clearly an Englishman. I still had some schoolboy French in those days and managed to order with a minimum of embarrassment. I was thrilled to be in the restaurant where so many of my literary heroes had dined and debated over the past century, but my female companion was not similarly impressed. As my salary in 1947 was two guineas (two pounds and two shillings) a week, I am baffled as to how I managed to pay the bill at the resplendent Cafe Royal, but I did somehow. After we arrived back in Bristol the young woman disappeared from sight. My love life in my teens was an unmitigated disaster. It wasn't until much later that I realized I was not alone in that condition. The puzzling contradiction was that on one hand I was a brash young newspaper reporter, knocking on people's doors and asking them personal questions about achievements or accidents, frequently against their wishes, and on the other hand I did not have the courage and verbal skill to make dates with the young women whom I fancied. With maturity, this ability improved somewhat but never to the point of finesse that many men possess.

Father began working in real estate with a wealthy man who was tolerant enough not to hold his dismal record against him. Later, as they began to prosper, together they formed a real estate company. For a surname, Father used his middle name, Martin, fearing repercussions from his past. We moved to a slightly better apartment, where we each had our room. Going our own ways, minding our own business, we lived happily together.

As my eighteenth birthday loomed, I became eligible for compulsory military service. This was not a prospect I welcomed, since I was so wrapped up in my career. I felt no desire to be a soldier, which almost certainly meant being part of the army of occupation in Germany, a necessary but uninteresting task. But at least I had the assurance that my newspaper was bound by law to reemploy me after my service, and I could take up my career again.

Two months after my eighteenth birthday, I became a private in the British Army and began three months of training as an infantryman at Bulford Barracks, Wiltshire, just within sight of Stonehenge. Training consisted mostly of route marches and "square-bashing"—drill and marching instructions. I don't recall learning much about actual warfare and I never mastered the art of shooting straight. I threw live grenades well—but then the penalty for failure with this activity would be death!

The route marches and cross-country running were over some of the loveliest countryside in England, and I never lost my love of Wiltshire. Every morning we passed the ancient Stonehenge monument in all its pristine glory. It hadn't yet become a world-famous tourist attraction and had no fences, car parks, or restaurants. We also could see in the distance the impressive

White Horses of Wiltshire, carved ten times greater than life into the hillsides.

After three months, I was dispatched to the Wiltshire Regiment stationed in Austria as part of the Allied occupation forces. The train journey down the Rhine shook me when I saw the tremendous extent of the damage to German cities, notably Cologne. I had thought Britain was heavily damaged by bombing raids, but it paled into insignificance compared to Germany. Nothing in 1948 had been rebuilt. Only the streets had been cleared and the railroads made workable. When I returned to Germany on holidays in the 1960s it was astonishing how fast and how well the reconstruction had been achieved, with no visible trace of war.

My next seventeen months were spent in Austria, alternating between stations in Klagenfurt in the south and Vienna. I preferred Vienna because several evenings a week I could go to performances by the world-renowned Vienna Philharmonic Orchestra and the State Opera Company. These concerts and operas went on long after the barracks closed, but my understanding commanding officer always gave me a late pass. I think he enjoyed classical music too. Not long after I left the army, I had the wonderful experience of seeing and hearing the great English composer Ralph Vaughan Williams, aged eighty, conduct the Halle Orchestra performing his *Sea Symphony* in the Free Trade Hall in Manchester.

I had hoped to spend my life in the army getting lots of fresh air and exercise, but my work experience spoiled that. Our regimental commanding officer needed a clerk/assistant. When he discovered my journalistic background in my records, including some speed in shorthand and typing, I was immediately marched off the parade ground and put behind a desk. My military service was notable for three things: losing my virginity, nearly being killed by friendly fire, and a narrow escape from imprisonment.

While walking in the village near Klagenfurt where we were based, I met a young woman who was very friendly. We went off into a field and somehow or other, after a lot of kissing, we made love. I was not very effective the first time and finished far too soon for her. Over the next few weeks, I overheard talk among my colleagues that she was the partner of a number of soldiers, and I never saw her again. The thought of sharing sexual favors with other men offended my youthful, puritanical soul. But we all have to start somewhere.

My brush with death came a few months later while my regiment was on maneuvers in the Karawanken Mountains between Austria and Yugoslavia. Although live ammunition was used in this training, we were not supposed to aim at people. My company was ordered to storm an imaginary machine-gun nest on a peak to the west, while artillery shelled a peak to the east. In real war, both would have been on one and the same peak. But the young officer in charge did not know his east from his west. He had us scale the wrong peak! We were nearly at the top when shells began to drop all around us. Luckily the terrain was very rugged and we threw ourselves into holes and crevices to avoid shrapnel, and fortunately there were no direct hits. I still have the sensation of fear and of pressing myself into the earth, wanting it to swallow me up. The experience left me grateful that I was never called upon to go into combat.

Just as I was posted to the Dorset Regiment in Austria, the military powers in London decided this should be Britain's first ski regiment. We were outfitted with expensive equipment, provided with local instructors, and tried out on the ample snowy slopes. On cross-country ski runs we had to carry mortars, machine guns, and ammunition on our backs—and we barely knew how to ski! Minor injuries were happening all the time; thus my colleagues hated this training because it disrupted their off-duty lives. In the 1940s and 1950s, skiing was still exclusively a wealthy person's sport, and these infantrymen in civilian life were laborers and truck drivers' assistants. Skiing held no glamour for them. It all came to a halt after a few months when an officer tackling a slope far too difficult for his level of skill was seriously injured. Considering all the injuries, and the extreme unpopularity of the mission, it was quickly dropped.

The cardinal sin of a British infantryman—and of all soldiers—is to fall asleep while on guard duty. Unfortunately my duties as company clerk did not excuse me from nighttime guard patrols around the camp. The night was split up into two hours on duty, and two hours off. That made sleep extremely difficult. For an eighteen-year-old who may have just had an exhausting day, staying awake in the early hours of the morning is a test of physical and mental stamina. But to be caught asleep while on guard earned immediate incarceration in a military prison.

Like my colleagues, I usually managed to hold out by constantly walking around—it was fatal to rest while on guard duty because sleep could overpower you in any position. One bitterly cold night, my last stint began at 4 a.m. when it was still dark. I was chilled and exhausted when I noticed the commanding officer's staff limousine parked on the parade ground. Temptation beckoned, and I got into the comfortable backseat. I planned to sit there for my last hour and of course, not sleep at all.

I awoke at 6:15 a.m. in broad daylight to find the entire regiment on the parade ground being mustered for morning inspection! Officers, commissioned and noncommissioned, surrounded the car, some of them a mere twenty feet away. Discovery meant real trouble. The guard commander must also have missed my not reporting back at 6 a.m. He would be searching for me too.

What to do? When the regiment was ordered to "about face," and everyone's eyes were in the opposite direction, I slipped out of the staff car and ran to the guardroom. The guard commander was asleep as he was entitled to be. When I awoke him, I mumbled something about my not noticing how time had flown. If someone had passed close to the staff car and seen me asleep in the backseat, I would have gone straight into confinement for several months. British military prisons were notorious for their harshness. The very thought of my narrow escape made me feel faint!

By early 1950, I was mustered out. Naively, I expected there to be some sort of home, with my father expecting me. So when I got off the train at Bristol, I called Father at our old apartment, only to get a message that the telephone was disconnected. I called Aunt Gwen, who said, cryptically but kindly, "He's married again. You'd better come and stay here." My books and papers were all lost. I was forced to drift again. So I never lived with my father after that. Gwen, the "earth mother" to the ubiquitous Humphry family, put me up for a while until I got back to work for the *Evening World* and had enough money to secure my own lodgings.

Chapter 4

ACQUIRING HOME AND FAMILY

W ITH MILITARY SERVICE BEHIND me at the age of twenty, I was free to start a journalistic career in earnest. I was fortunate. By accident of birth date, I'd been obliged to serve only twenty months—during the previous decade, many men had spent up to six years in military service, a disastrous slice out of their young lives. I, however, now had a certain personality maturity, a veneer of education and sophistication, and a more focused perspective of where I was going with my life.

My first decision was not to return to sports reporting. It was too trivial and repetitive. I preferred to jump straight into "hard news" reporting. My goal was to be a top news reporter within five years.

The *Bristol Evening World* was an excellent training ground. It aimed at bright writing, had a smart typographical appearance, expected scoops from its reporters, and was in fierce competition with the *Bristol Evening Post*. The news staff under Reginald Eason was relatively young and recently demobilized from the services—and thus worldly. All were hungry for fame and fortune in the postwar era. Most were experienced journalists, ten or fifteen years older than I, and willingly helped train this youngster in the wiles and intricacies of cutthroat journalism. Viewing the press since the 1980s, it's hard to see much in the way of commercial media competition and journalistic rivalry today. But in cities across America and Britain there used to be two or three papers in each community fighting it out for circulation and advertising. In the 1960s and 1970s television and radio siphoned off the cream of the advertising money, causing the number of newspapers mostly to drop to one per city. Today, even in those cities where there are still two, generally they have special trade agreements that reduce competition.

In the 1950s, press competition was back to the ferocity it had possessed during the notorious newspaper wars of the 1930s. Newspaper owners were staking out claims to the new postwar prosperity. At the same time, they were keeping a fearful eye on the growing power of television. At the *Evening World* we confidently expected to drive our press rival into the ground. Arrogantly, we thought we had the most scoops, the best layout, the best sports, and so on. We *had* to come out on top. However, those who owned and managed the finances of the paper saw it differently. Control of the *Evening World* soon passed to the *Evening Post*. The merger took all the fun out of "our paper," and the more adventurous members of the staff soon left for London to test their talents in bigger fields of journalism. (A few years later, the *World* followed other papers into extinction, leaving the *Post* as the only evening newspaper.)

I knew that I was not ready for London; instead, I applied by letter to the entire list of major provincial newspapers in the north of England. All my life I had lived in southern England. I wanted to have a taste of what lay in the north. To my delight, I received the offer of a job from the *Manchester Evening News*. At that time it was the largest provincial evening newspaper in the country. The same company owned the *Manchester Guardian*, later renamed the *Guardian*.

The job offered—at eight guineas a week (eight pounds and eight shillings sterling)—was somewhat unusual. It involved covering the affairs of a newly built township named Wythenshawe on the outskirts of Manchester. Almost all the residents of Wythenshawe had formerly lived in the poor or slum areas of the inner city, which were fast being torn down because of unsanitary conditions. Though these residents were suddenly presented with a better standard of life, there was a downside to their nice new homes: they needed to create a fresh community spirit. Shops, schools, and churches were built as quickly as possible but could never keep up with the more easily erected homes that were needed for the so-called "baby boomers." In his letter of appointment, the editor warned that "covering Wythenshawe and district will be without doubt a very tough proposition."

The *Evening News* supplied me with a motorcycle to travel around the sprawling housing estate, picking up news and instantly telephoning it to the paper's head office in central Manchester. My problem was that there was hardly any news to be found! People were merely sleeping in Wythenshawe and traveling elsewhere to work, and even to play. It was the typical "dormitory town." The community lacked the usual infrastructure of clubs, libraries, pubs, and church groups, making news extremely hard to find. Crime is the staple diet of the media, but there was hardly any in Wythenshawe. None of the residents was wealthy, and there were as yet no jewelers' shops or banks for criminals to rob.

For hours every weekday morning I would ride around, in the rain or sunshine, watching new buildings being erected or talking to the handful of clergymen who mostly had no churches as yet. They needed someone to talk to as much as I did! The only way to communicate with politicians or youth leaders was to visit them in the evenings when they had traveled home from work. I would meet with them for hours, hoping some nuggets worthy of a story would emerge. Getting news out of sterile Wythenshawe was like pulling teeth. Sometimes the elements helped me; once I was riding a bridge over the River Mersey and out of the corner of my eye saw men putting sandbags in front of a weir (a small dam). Dumping my motorcycle on the sidewalk, I ran down to the riverbank and gleaned information for a front-page story about the melting winter snows causing such pressure on the weir that it was in serious danger of breaking and causing extensive flooding. Earthy and worthy stuff for a local paper!

Another time I was sitting in a cafe—extremely bored, not having telephoned a story to my paper for two whole days—when the gas station on the other side of the road exploded before my eyes. People ran for their lives as flames shot upwards into the sky and smoke billowed into the road. First I called the fire brigade and then my paper. Yet such surprises were rare moments of news-gathering good luck.

Up to the time I joined the Manchester paper at twenty-one, I had never used alcohol. Beer, the traditional English drink, had offended my taste buds. Stupidly, I let this fact slip at the reporters' table one day, inciting the veteran reporters, unknown to me, to do something about it. To them it was heresy to be a journalist among them and not drink. For example, how could a reporter interview people in a pub if he didn't drink? One evening after work, they took me to their favorite watering hole, very slyly plying me with drink after drink, masked by lots of conviviality and story telling. By the end of the evening I was drunk. In the pouring rain, I staggered out of the pub and promptly fell into the gutter in the city's main square, Piccadilly. For a length of time not known to me I lay in the curbside of the road with water running over me. I tried to get up but could not. Then a taxi pulled alongside and two senior reporters picked me up and threw me on its floor. As they had no idea what to do with me, one of them, Peter Beresford, took me to his home and tossed me on a spare bed. And he had me back at the newsroom desk the next day by the regulation time of 8 a.m. Though I have sometimes since been tipsy, the demeaning memory of that wet experience in the Piccadilly gutter has stopped me from ever again being drunk and incapable. For the last ten years, for medical reasons, I stopped drinking altogether. But I do miss the preprandial whiskey and wine with dinner.

A bad habit that I feel grateful to have avoided is smoking cigarettes, cigars, and pipes. As a boy during the war, I watched people—almost everybody—smoking heavily. It can be forgiven by the need to calm their nerves when their lives were in danger, or worrying about a loved one somewhere in the conflict. I watched—fascinated—as people inhaled and then blew the smoke out of their noses. Of course, nobody knew in those days how dangerous tar and nicotine are for one's health. But the secondhand smoke often stung my eyes. Some instinct told me that smoking was not only a waste of money but also was not natural. Even more depressing was witnessing people—as the saying goes—"coughing their lungs out" in the mornings. The smokers would openly blame their nicotine habit yet never did anything about it. Journalists are—or were—inveterate smokers; some could not write a word without a "fag" hanging from their lips. Fortunately, I never succumbed, despite the fact that it was not until just before the 1960s that medical scientists warned positively that tobacco smoke was carcinogenic.

Over a long career as a newspaper reporter, I conducted many strange interviews, but none ever started out as badly as one I did soon after joining the *Manchester Evening News*. A number of homes were due to be demolished for street widening. Sent to get some local inhabitants' comments, I knocked on the first door to ask what the occupant felt about this upheaval. A woman of about forty answered the door.

"Good Morning! I'm Derek Humphry, a reporter for the *Evening News*."

"One of your delivery trucks knocked down and killed my husband."

Once I had got over my surprise at this remarkable response, I expressed my condolences and asked how long ago this had happened. Two years, I was told. Even though there was still a strong undercurrent of hostility from the widow, I decided to try the interview. I knew that my ruthless news editor would not accept this accident as a reason for failure. As it turned out, when I switched the conversation to the future of the street, the widow was happy to be interviewed and chattered on quite cheerfully.

During my two years in Wythenshawe, I uncovered only one story of national importance. The Manchester Girl Guides' Association expelled from its membership a guide captain who announced she was also a Communist. The association felt that the guide's promise "to do my duty to God and the Queen" could not be sworn by a Communist, an ideology based on atheism. The guide's response was that the loss was more that of the guide movement's than hers. This was in 1953, when the Cold War was at its height and McCarthyism in America was emerging. My story made national and international headlines.

Hard Hunt For News

Even in a backwater like Wythenshawe, a reporter occasionally came across connections with famous people. From the police

blotter I picked up the name of a young man killed in a motorcycle accident: Hans-Peter Einstein. Wondering if he might be
related to the discoverer of relativity, the great scientist Albert
Einstein, I went to his home address to check. Hans-Peter turned
out to be the great-great-nephew of the famous scientist. He,
too, had fled from Nazi persecution in 1939. A remote family
connection, but enough to justify a story.

My desperate everyday hunt for news fine-tuned my powers of observation and improved my interviewing techniques.
On my ability to extract a printable quote from a person laid
the success or failure of a story. As for writing, that was no
strain because the *Evening News* printed few news items longer than three or four paragraphs. It was more akin to writing
telegrams.

I also did some "creative writing" for the newspaper when
it needed "Letters to the Editor." Every Friday afternoon, all
the reporters were asked to read the issues for the past week and
invent letters purporting to come from concerned readers. We
dreamed up names and addresses for these apocryphal missives,
and the ethics were never questioned. It was all part of the business of making a living; if a page had to be filled with letters
between the advertisements, then it had to be done. And if I am
any judge, things haven't changed in this regard. I would bet that
many letters to the editor printed in magazines and newspapers
today are phony as well.

Competition with the rival *Evening Chronicle* was ruthless.
If you were assigned to a story at which the *Chronicle* was also
present, you had to telephone the news to your paper first, especially an important public announcement, a court sentence, or an
election result. In the 1950s, public telephones in Britain were
fairly scarce. If your rival got to the only one in the area first
and remained on the line for twenty or so minutes, you were

scooped. Those were the days when evening newspapers printed updated editions every hour. To be scooped in those days could mean the loss of your job. Editors were pitiless. Back in Bristol, a seasoned reporter had taught me a trick about telephones that I often put into practice in Manchester. The speaking cup could be easily unscrewed from the handset. Inside was a disc of mica. Slip the mica into your pocket, reassemble the equipment in a flash, and the phone was out of order. When I was ready to telephone my story, I returned to the telephone kiosk, covertly replaced the disc, and scooped the opposition.

Within a year, I had milked Wythenshawe for every story it had, and pounced on any new ones the second they appeared. I was desperate to know what to do with myself during the long, damp, cold winter days. Fortunately, I became friendly with a Methodist minister, who was also bored in the afternoons. We would sit for hours in the comfortable study of his home talking about books and literature. He collected first editions by hunting through used bookstores.

This enforced indolence came crashing to a halt when one day I opened an envelope delivered to the Beehive Cafe where I hung out. It contained this note:

Dear Humphry,

I have been watching your work closely for the past few months and the thing that strikes me forcibly is the dwindling amount of copy you are sending and the poor quality of much of it. I enclose your efforts for seven days. Coverage of an area in which live 70,000 people merits more than this and I am considering the position. Quite obviously you are not one hundred per cent employed and it may be necessary to widen the scope of your area.

Alternately it may be necessary to move you to another district.

Yours truly,

T E Henry, Editor

When I had recovered from the embarrassment of this rebuke, I realized that perhaps this could be the way to escape from my loathsome exile in boring Wythenshawe. I longed to be back among fellow reporters, aching for the camaraderie around the big table of the *News* office in Cross Street. I yearned for some big-time news work. So I telephoned for an appointment with Mr. Henry. I described to him my efforts over the past year, having typed out a list of everyone I could remember calling to see. And I reminded him that he would not allow me to rent the smallest office. Working from cafes did not make it easy for people to contact me. He was impressed by my diligence and said that he would begin to look for a replacement, but asked me to nurse Wythenshawe for a while longer. The paper had also decided to build a small office there, but it was unlikely to be ready in time for me.

While I was covering the Wythenshawe and north Cheshire beat, I now know that I missed one of the most significant stories of the century. Or perhaps it was kept from me on the grounds of national security. My routine inspection of police blotters in the area during June 1954 did not show me that a man called Alan Turing had committed suicide. Anyway, who was Turing, apart from a local convicted homosexual? Today, for two reasons, he has a street named after him, Alan Turing Way, and a statue in a Manchester's Sackville Park.

Alan Turing invented the computer. In 1937, he published in a tiny Scottish mathematical journal a paper called "Computable

Numbers," which today is acknowledged to have outlined exactly how a computer would work. Unfortunately, the technology did not then exist to put Turing's advanced ideas into practice.

Secondly, Turing's individual contribution to winning World War II is inestimable. As well as being the most original mathematical genius of his time, he had been the leading cryptographer at the secret Bletchley Park, cracking German military and naval codes. He led the team that, from their little offices in a country mansion, fought the Battle of the Atlantic as German submarines tried to starve Britain into submission. His work on the Enigma coding system was brilliant. Historians have speculated that Turing may have contributed more to victory in the war than any other one person. (The best biography of Turing I have read is *Alan Turing: The Enigma* by Andrew Hodges [Simon & Schuster, 1983.]) Knowledge of Turing's cryptographic work, plus the Bletchley Park's smashing of the Enigma code, was kept secret until the 1980s. But at the time of his death, he was a Reader at Manchester University, working on the development of computers. Turing also knew a great deal about British and American coding systems at the time when we were deep in the Cold War with Russia, thus I suspect the authorities kept his death secret. It went completely unremarked. Turing suffered greatly as a result of his homosexuality, being convicted of the offense of "gross indecency," put on probation, and ordered—in the retrograde medical thinking in the 1950s—to be treated with drugs that were supposed to make him heterosexual. "Organo-Therapic treatment" it was called; all it did was make him impotent, grow larger breasts, and be deeply unhappy. A solitary man, his sufferings at the time are unknown but can be imagined. Then, like Snow White, he dipped an apple into a container of cyanide, bit into it, and died. He was forty-two, his eminent place in world history not known publicly for another thirty years.

There was, to be sure, another facet to my life in that otherwise unremarkable place. Dull Wythenshawe was not without certain charming assets.

ROMANTIC INTERVIEW

It began when I arranged by telephone to interview a young woman who was active in the youth movement of Wythenshawe. Jean Crane was, I had heard, trying to unite the young persons' groups in the area to formulate a census of public opinion on the quality of life in the new township. Our interview took place in a youth club after a meeting, and we talked animatedly for some time. I was immediately attracted to Jean, who was just twenty-one, tall, blonde, and sturdily built, and had an openness of countenance that portrayed a determined, wholesome character. She was not what you would call pretty but was a handsome person. Somewhat shy, I did not ask her for a date at that meeting. Instead, I sent to her home a letter of thanks for the interview and in a footnote said: "As you appreciate good music, would you care to join me at a concert? I enclose a spare ticket, hoping to meet you there."

A few days later (March 18, 1953, to be exact) I took my two shillings and sixpence seat in the Free Trade Hall. As the French National Orchestra was tuning up, Jean strode in and sat down. On the program was César Franck's Sixth Symphony, and during the intermission, Jean and I went on at length about its beauty and the dynamism with which it had been conducted. Over coffee in a cafe afterwards, conversation turned to talk about our beliefs and our dreams. Soon our romance was off and running on that first date. It turned out that in addition to our physical attraction, we shared similar credos. Most of the young women

I had previously dated did not think about politics or life in the same way.

An only child, Jean was born in 1932 in the economically depressed slum area of Hulme, Manchester, and her parents had a hard fight to make even the barest living. Her father was mostly out of work, and her mother brought in some money cleaning offices. At the first opportunity to escape from the grime and poverty of Hulme, the couple had moved to Wythenshawe so that Jean could attend a pleasantly situated school nearby. During World War II, Jean's father found occasional work, but a harsh childhood followed by twenty years of almost continual unemployment had soured him.

Sidney Crane was virtually unemployable by reason of his cynical attitudes. It also did not help that his bitterness at his fate in life had turned him into a Communist. In truth, he was more of an armchair Marxist than an activist; he loved to talk about how the world would be fairer under Communism, but he did next to nothing to help achieve this Utopia.

Typically, if campaign leaflets had to be delivered, he would bribe teenage Jean to tramp from door-to-door with them. But he was unable to stop talking about how badly life had treated him and how Communism was the solution. Naturally enough, employers boycotted him. At the age of fifty, the government employment authorities permanently stamped him as "unemployable"—meaning he no longer had to seek work in order to draw benefits—and he lapsed into a beneficent retirement. From my wider observations in Manchester, Sid was by no means the only man in his age group whose work ethic was not allowed to flourish, or was destroyed, by the Great Depression of the 1930s.

Jean paid only lip service to her father's left-wing views. She had her own ideas about how people should help each other—through community service. When we met, she was chairperson of Wythenshawe Youth Council. In 1950, she had been elected "Miss Wythenshawe," which was not so much a beauty contest (although the person had to be presentable) as it was a contest to become someone willing to open bazaars and fetes, present prizes at sporting events, and so forth. The fledgling township had no mayor or similar personage to act as this civic functionary. For twelve months, Jean had devoted many evenings and weekends as the township's ambassador. Newspaper photographs show her elegant and self-possessed in a gown and huge garden-party hat at celebrations and carnivals. But her real interest was working in youth clubs.

Jean and I shared a love of tramping over the hills and dales, exploring the countryside surrounding Manchester. It was such a relief to be able to leave the grimy industrial city on my motorcycle, with Jean riding behind me. Within an hour we'd be walking along some of the most remote and beautiful country in Britain. Our first tramp was over Kinder Scout, a small mountain, on a rugged route that was part of the 250-mile-long Pennine Way between Derbyshire and Northumberland. By now, I was madly in love with her and after only three weeks of courtship asked her to marry me. She must have been just as crazy, for she accepted on the spot. We fixed the marriage for three weeks later!

My salary at the newspaper had by now risen to ten pounds a week. That made it possible to rent an apartment and prepare for a new phase of my life. Neither Jean nor I was interested in a church or formal wedding. Instead we were married one morning in a quiet civil ceremony at the Registry Office in All Saints Square, Manchester. My father's soft-top Railton Straight Eight car could seat only four—Jean's parents in the back—so Jean rode to her marriage on my lap in the front passenger seat. Jean's parents and my father were our sole witnesses. Then we five had a jovial lunch together and went home. I must confess that I have never understood how an elaborate, expensive wedding adds anything to a marriage other than a lot of work, emotional strain, and sometimes debt. About that time, I reported on the late-in-life second marriage of Herbert Morrison, a famous British politician, to a younger woman in Rochdale, Lancashire. When I asked him how many guests were going to be at his wedding, he quipped: "None. That would be an intrusion into private grief!"

Marriage made me even keener to get ahead with my career. Thus, while still working for the *Evening News*, I spent my twenty-fifth year hunting for a reporting job on a national newspaper. I targeted the *Daily Express*, the *Daily Mail*, the *Daily Mirror*, and the *Daily Telegraph*, keeping up a barrage of letters to their news editors (called *city* editors in the US) to remind them of the great talent they were ignoring. Finally, one day, the *Daily Mail* summoned me for an interview. The news editor, Ronnie Jeans, accepted my credentials and liked me as a person but said that I must also be vetted by the editor, Howard French.

Ushered into the editor's office, at first I could not see anybody. Then Mr. Jeans addressed a copy of the *Times* newspaper behind which somebody wearing dark pinstripe trousers was reading with his back to a window on the far side of the elegantly appointed office.

"This is Derek Humphry, Mr. French, whom I would like to take on our reporting staff." A pregnant silence followed. Mr. Jeans and I looked at each other expectantly.

Abruptly the *Times* was snapped shut, and a tall man with a military bearing and a handlebar mustache appeared from behind the newspaper. He barked: "Any mistakes and you're fired. Go." End of successful job interview!

I had already met enough eccentric people in journalism not to be bothered by an oddball character like French—albeit a powerful man—so within a month I was the youngest reporter on the staff of the *Daily Mail* at a weekly salary of fifteen guineas a week. (A guinea was one pound and one shilling. There had not been a guinea coin for years. A leftover from history, it was in those days fashionable to speak of "guineas." It is no longer a unit of currency in the UK. Yet, as fifteen guineas was fifteen shillings more than fifteen pounds, who was I to complain of this anachronism?)

I enjoyed the quality reporting at the *Daily Mail* and must have fitted in well because I still have a letter from the dreadful Howard French six months after starting work, offering congratulations and a raise of two guineas.

By this time, our first child, Edgar, arrived. Jean and I had moved with the baby into a little row house, Number 3 Barwick Place, Sale, Cheshire, on the Manchester border. It was a modest home, with two rooms upstairs and two down and the lavatory outside in the yard, typical of the Victorian housing built to accommodate the workers flowing from the countryside into the towns during the previous century.

It had been offered cheaply because a long-term town council plan said this house and others were to be demolished for city redevelopment. I was advised that this would not take place for many years. (It is still there fifty years later, albeit remodeled!) Because of the planning blight, I was able to buy it for five hundred pounds, selling a motorcycle I owned to pay half and borrowing the rest from the seller. Within two years I had repaid the entire balance. Edgar was born in Withington Hospital, Manchester, in 1954. We named him after our two favorite French Post-Impressionist painters, Edgar (Degas) and Vincent (Van Gogh). In 1956, our second son, Clive, was born at Barwick Place. When the doctor came through the door to assist the delivery, he saw a birthday party in progress and commented: "That's a bit soon, isn't it?"

We all laughed, for by a combination of biology and coincidence Edgar had been born on the same day—February 6—two years earlier. You could not have found a happier young married couple in the whole of England. With my wife and children, I was proud to have put my life together successfully, albeit in a low key. What a contrast to the mess my own childhood had been!

Jean and I were idealists. For instance, in 1955 we joined the Commonwealth of World Citizens, a beautiful but outlandish group that wanted to make everybody a world citizen to reduce the likelihood of world wars. It was a popular idea in the 1950s, with people still reeling from World War II and willing to look at any way to avoid another. A man called Garry Davis drew extensive public attention when he was the first person to declare himself a world citizen; his declaration was followed by a huge "people's conference" in Geneva to debate the idea. When the philosopher and writer Dr. Hugh J Schonfield launched the Commonwealth of World Citizens in 1950, it attracted hundreds of members, including Jean and me.

In August 1956, I attended the Constituent Assembly in the Temple of Peace and Health in Cardiff, Wales, which also housed the United Nations Association. Nothing that was said there has remained in my memory—but I do recall a strangely ironic event. The first night in my hotel I was aroused by the roar of heavy traffic. From my window I could see dozens of military trucks on the move, along with tanks and heavy artillery on their carriers. The convoys continued for three nights (never by day). They were secretly heading to Cardiff docks—but why? There was no hint of any forthcoming war so far as I knew. The answer came a short while later when the UK and France, with Israel's connivance, invaded Egypt on October 29, 1956, to regain control of the Suez Canal, which President Gamal Nasser had seized and nationalized. It was a short war because US President Eisenhower told the British and the French very firmly they must withdraw immediately. The Soviets took advantage of the ensuing chaos to invade Hungary. How strange that I was at a peace conference at the same time that the instruments of a new war were passing under my window!

The following year, I made a speech to the Commonwealth meeting in Manchester, of which—amazingly—I still have the original typescript. Fifty years later, I still stand by what I said then as a twenty-seven-year-old, but the experience was a hard lesson in trying to turn ideals into realities. The Commonwealth lasted ten years and faded away in 1960. To this day I remain loyal to the ideal of world citizenship—and to a small extent have succeeded, being a passport-carrying citizen of both the United States of America and Europe.

Another example of our idealism came with the adoption of Stephen. I had written an article for the *Manchester Evening News* on the overcrowding in the city's orphanages. There was nothing wrong with the way the children were cared for—there were just too many, and almost nobody was willing to adopt them. Usually adoptive parents want babies so that they can be raised by their standards and customs. The children I was writing about were over three years old, and many were black or of mixed race. Jean and I were considering having a third—and last—child when one day she declared that there was no point in bringing another child into the world when there were so many neglected kids in orphanages. (Manchester, by the way, had an enlightened policy of keeping the kids in groups of eight to ten in large houses with a married couple in charge. There was no "warehousing.") Jean suggested we adopt a boy around three to four years old; I agreed.

We applied to the local children's department in 1960, and they promptly sent a social worker to assess us at home. When

we were asked about our faiths, we replied that were not believ-
ers in any religion. I thought this would spoil our chances, but as
it turned out it did not. Jean and I must have said that we did not
mind what race the child was, but we preferred a boy of around
four so as to fit in with our existing children. I can see on the
acceptance letter, which I still have, the final words penned by
the social worker: "Accepted for a colored child."

We were asked to consider a four-year-old boy of mixed race
called Stephen. We were told at once that he was the unwanted son
of a prostitute in Moss Side, the city's infamous ghetto (in recent
years rebuilt and cleaned up). His father was unknown. A more
difficult launch into a tough world is hard to imagine. When he
was born in Wythenshawe Hospital a few days before Christmas
1957, his mother took one look at him—so we were told—and as
he was white she refused to pick him up. Her previous three children had been black. Stephen was what West Indian people call a
"pinkie." White in complexion with some Negro features, there
are many such in the Caribbean islands, where they are treated
just the same as a black person. I have also seen similar-looking
people in the dock cities of Cardiff and Liverpool, where sailors
of many races come and go. For reasons we shall never know,
Stephen's mother left the hospital without him, and the nurses
named him Stephen because it was now Christmas Day, and in
Europe, many refer to Christmas as St. Stephen's Day.

For the next three years, the Manchester social workers tried
to reunite Stephen with his mother. She took him back when
he was one, but a few weeks later the social workers checked
and found him filthy, with bedsores, and seriously undernourished. They took him back into their care. The following year
they tried again, providing his mother with a small apartment,
furniture, and money. Soon after, they found him once again
undernourished, with pneumonia and incipient rickets. They

removed him from her care for the last time, settling him into a miniature orphanage. His behavior was unruly and destructive and was driving those in charge of him to despair. A psychiatrist insisted that the only remedy for this wildness was a normal home environment.

Twice, other married couples took him home "on trial" because adoption by law can only occur after a successful six-month period, at the end of which both prospective parents and the child must want the adoption made permanent. Twice, Stephen was sent back to the city's care as the married couples found that they could not cope with his rebellious behavior. Each time he must have thought he had found a loving family, only to be robbed. The practice for intended adoption was for us to visit Stephen in his foster care home and see whether there was affinity and friendship. We liked him from the start. Then he came to stay with us for the occasional weekend. Finally he came to live with us for the six-month trial period. Stephen was a handful. He wet the bed and was disobedient, a totally free spirit. He ran over people's flower beds as if they did not exist. We called him "our little Communist" from his habit of treating other children's' toys as if they were his own, and he gave out anything he owned. Each evening we had to sort out the toys and books that were in our household but were not ours and go around the neighborhood returning them and collecting his possessions.

But gradually, through Jean's patience, he calmed down and settled in with the family for the next few years. The troubles started again when he reached puberty at a point in time when racism reared its ugly head in America and Britain. The riots in American cities were big television news in Britain. Riots in England were not as violent and bloody but bad enough. Schoolchildren can be hateful to one another at times. As the editor of the local newspaper, I lived in Billericay, a white, middle-class

town. Stephen's classmates—alerted by all the television coverage of race news—noticed that he looked different from them.
They began to taunt him about his looks and racial origins to the
extent that he became extremely angry and frustrated. Running
away from school one day, for instance, he demanded of Jean:
"What am I? Black or white?" Jean replied: "You are a human
being, as good as anyone else. And remember, we chose to bring
you into our family. That's how much we love you."

An additional upset was the Vietnam War, battle scenes
from which were a constant feature on the nightly news. One
clip showed black soldiers right in the firing line, causing Stephen to ask me: "Why do the black people have to do all the
fighting in wars?" If I recall, I tried to explain that soldiers were
not only black people—there were plenty of whites as well, and
he should realize that America had a significant population of
people descended from earlier African slaves. But the question
was just another reminder of the racial identity problems with
which Stephen struggled. All teenagers have growing-up problems; unlucky Stephen had also to cope with being adopted and
of mixed-race origin.

Chapter 5

A CURIOUS REUNION

ONE DAY MY MOTHER suddenly walked back into my life. For twenty years there had been absolutely no contact between us, by her choice. Now, from Australia she had contacted the police in Bristol asking them to inform her two sons of her address and requesting them to make contact. With his residual memories, so many of which were unpleasant, Garth was cool to her request. I had no memory of what she had been like, so I was keener to see her, if only out of natural curiosity. Immediately I wrote off to the address in Lismore, New South Wales. I cannot remember what I said in my letter but I still have her reply, dated April 20, 1953:

> My Dear Son,
>   Received your welcome letter and your good news. My gosh! To think both my sons are married. . . . I have never liked this country; part of it was because of you two, away from me. While I have a nice home—mine, not John's—and saved some money, do you think it would

be worthwhile to come home (to England) and try to get a business or maybe a farm for John? . . . I cannot bear the idea of never seeing you. I have lost so much of you. I should never have come here; the loneliness was awful. . . .

All my love, your Mother.

For the next year we engaged in regular correspondence. I still have all her letters, which are littered with phrases such as "It's the only goal I've had, hoping to see you boys again" and "wanting to see you has undermined my health." She speaks of the surprise the rest of the family must feel at her popping up again. "Now I'm a much happier person and looking forward to the time of coming home and seeing my sons, daughters-in-law, and grandchildren." She commented that this made her sound "like an old woman." In fact she was forty-three.

After selling everything in Australia, Mother, her husband, John Eden, a tropical fruit inspector for the state government, and their eight-year-old son, Sean, sailed from Sydney. When their ship neared England, I took time off from the *Evening News* and boarded the train to Southampton Harbor to meet her off the steamship *Esperance Bay*. The prospect of meeting my mother consciously for the first time at age twenty-four was a daunting and strange experience. Would the chemistry be good? If not, what would happen then? I had no idea what she looked like, nor had I seen any photographs. Anyway, curiosity overwhelmed any doubts and fears; as the ship docked. I was waiting at the bottom of the gangplank. She was petite and slim with brunette hair and delicate features. We made some small talk as she, her husband, and small son transferred their baggage to the London train. Then she and I had lunch together in the dining car as the train raced northwards. "You look just like me," she said with obvious gratification.

As we exchanged all our family news it became apparent that she was much undecided about how to resettle her family in England. Her ideas ranged from acquiring a farm to purchasing a public house, delicatessen, or antique store. She had made a fair amount of money in Australia buying antique furniture and bric-a-brac in the city and trucking it to outback farms and remote communities to resell at a profit. Much of our conversation was trivial, yet forty years later I remember her recurrent theme: she was still young and energetic and was going to become a successful businesswoman in England.

After settling Mother and her family in a small London hotel, I took the train back to my own family and work in Manchester. The next day I was able to tell Jean that our reunion had been a good one although there was still a long way to go before Mother and I truly got to know each other. "She's too absorbed in getting the family settled to be able to relax and talk," I explained. That turned out to be a prophetic comment because Mother never settled down.

First, John and she agreed to buy a delicatessen in London. Then they backed off. Hating the onset of the English winter, yearning for the sunshine, they set off back to Australia by ship. When they reached Sydney, John disembarked, but Mother immediately turned straight around with Sean and sailed back to England. This was puzzling, but obviously the family was torn with indecision. John had been born in England and emigrated to Australia as a small boy, but having taken a second look at his birthplace as a mature person, he decided he preferred Australia.

Mother's loyalties were divided between her two sons in England and her husband thousands of miles away. Judging from her letters, she was also torn between what she called "the loneliness of Australia," with its beautiful warm weather, and England's homely but dismal climate.

Mother now began arranging to purchase or lease a public house in London from a major brewing company. Once again, as the deal came near to closure, she backed off, saying that the work would be too rigorous compared to the financial rewards. I paid occasional visits to her in London, and we corresponded at other times. We got on well, but there was never any overt affection shown on either of our parts. I assumed that a hug or a kiss would follow as our relationship grew closer. She was more comfortable expressing her affection in writing.

All of her letters, even the last one, ended with "Lots of love from your mother." John refused to return to England, so Mother booked passage to Australia for herself and little Sean to sail on the *Strathaird* from Tilbury in October, escaping the English winter. Each time she departed we had a mutual under-standing that she would contact me from Australia and that at some point I would travel there. I was interested in working for an Australian newspaper to broaden my experience and applied to several in Sydney. Each editor replied that if I turned up they would consider employing me. I related this to Mother, explain-ing that I had not decided to immigrate permanently to Australia but would keep the option open.

She sailed away and I settled down to wait for the usual air-mail letter. When it arrived, it bore a local London postmark and said in part, "I don't know whether you will be pleased or not, but Sean and I are back in London. We got off the ship in Port Said and got back here on 8th of November." Clearly Mother's erratic behavior signaled that something was wrong, but I was too immature and too heavily involved in my own domestic and pro-fessional affairs to discover what the trouble was. In addition to our living two hundred miles apart, whenever we met she didn't seem able to confide in or to listen to me. Instead, she incessantly talked about unrealistic plans. Even more troubling, during the entire year she spent—with breaks—in England, she never visited my home to meet my wife and son. When I asked her to come she always protested that she either did not have the time or the health to travel north, which was a straightforward train ride. I suspected that it had more to do with an unhappy visit to Garth's home. Known for her sharp tongue, Garth's wife had rebuked Mother for "abandoning your son," and this had wounded her. She probably could not bear the prospect of a second attack, even though I knew Jean would not have been that unkind and tactless, despite the fact that for twenty years she had not made the slightest contact with her English sons—not even a greeting card.

Shortly after returning to London from their halfway trip, she announced that she and Sean were setting off again for Australia, swearing that this was definitely the last time. She promised to write me as soon as she had relocated, and in return I promised to keep in touch. Perhaps I would join her soon as a working journalist. But months without a letter from her turned into years, and I never heard from her again. I discussed with Garth the prospect of looking for her. Perhaps she was dead, I suggested. Maybe there was a tragedy? I wanted to resolve the dilemma out of a natural curiosity to know what had happened to my kith and kin. He, however, adamantly refused. "I don't care what has happened to her," he said.

Leading a full and rewarding life of my own, I dropped the matter for the time being. Besides, even though I did not know how to contact her (perhaps she had gone elsewhere than Australia?), Mother could easily contact us by letter or telephone. But even though no envelope arrived and no phone call came, it was by no means the end of the story.

Chapter 6

REPORTER AT LARGE

WORKING ON THE *DAILY Mail* brought me under the influence of a remarkable journalist, James A. Lewthwaite. Scores of newspapermen and -women around the world were trained by Jimmy. I was fortunate enough to come under his tutelage from 1955–1960, and we were to become good friends. True, our friendship was due in part to the fact that we lived close to each other. I owned a little car, whereas Jimmy did not drive. It suited him to take me out drinking at Manchester Press Club after work so that I could drop him home afterwards. Jimmy was meticulous about the sort and quality of the beer he drank. It had to be McEwen's Ale with a certain amount of sediment in the bottom. Without that quantity of sediment, Jimmy would hand the bottle back to the bartender. Nobody could pour his beer for him, and if it did not fill up with the right amount of frothy head, or have the proper color, back that one would go as well. Jimmy had an authoritative manner with which bartenders didn't choose to quarrel. Only when all his standards were met would Jimmy quaff his beer.

Jimmy, a short, stocky man with clipped gray hair and horn-rimmed glasses, was totally averse to anything relating to exercise. When not working at his desk at night, he was either reading, watching cricket, or sitting at a bar—anything sedentary. He loved to tell the story of his predecessor, just as unathletic in his habits, who had—so Jimmy claimed—the dubious honor of being the only *Daily Mail* journalist to live until the pensionable age of sixty-five. When he retired, the management gave him a push lawnmower as a token of their esteem. Within a month, the retiree dropped dead under the strain of mowing his lawn. Jimmy loved to say that was how the company kept the pension fund profitable.

Jimmy was night news editor of the northern edition of the *Daily Mail*, and I, as the youngest reporter on the paper, also worked mostly at night. Already nearly sixty years old when we first met, Jimmy was the quintessential "hard-nosed" British journalist, noted for his tremendous persistence and ingenuity in handling difficult stories. He had been a national newspaper reporter for several top-flight newspapers in his younger days, and there was nothing he didn't know about the quirks of journalism or the oddities of journalists.

Jimmy not only knew how to get stories but how to write them as well—crisply, factually, and safe from libel. Even if he hated the story you had just given him, and despite his gruff Cumberland manner, without embarrassing you he could still tell you just where it had gone wrong and how it could be corrected. Sometimes his method of criticism was by exaggeration. Once I telephoned in a late-night story about a woman being stabbed. On returning to the office, I asked Jimmy what he thought of my account, which had been done hastily to catch the midnight edition. "It had about two gallons too much blood in it, old man," he commented. (He always referred to men affectionately as "old man.") Jimmy was also famous for droll, understated comments. My favorite example was when I was driving him home one night and had to make an extremely rapid stop. Jimmy, who had a cigarette permanently between his lips, was flung forward into the windshield, and the burning cigarette was rammed into his mouth. As he lurched back into his seat, he regurgitated the cigarette and muttered, "That was a bit sudden, old man!" No cuss word or anger or criticism.

Journalists have big egos. That is how they stand the uneven pace of their work and the daily public scrutiny of their efforts. Whenever Jimmy heard journalists boasting of their prowess, he made his favorite leavening comment, "Old man, it's the quality of the copy which you put in my basket in the evening which really counts." One senior journalist on the paper, Harry Procter, was known for the quality of his work though he drank more than was good for him. While he was drunk, Harry was unable to pound the keys of a typewriter. But we knew he could still dictate beautiful stories. As the hours ticked by and Harry had still not put his night's typed copy in the basket, Jimmy would call me over. "Take him out of the office to the nearest telephone box, push him in, give him the money to call the office, and see that he dictates his story to the copytakers." It always worked.

Harry wouldn't have kept his job as long as he did without this stratagem of Jimmy's. Unfortunately, even this did not save Harry. He was eventually fired for persistent drunkenness. This has always been a problem in the highly competitive field of journalism, leading to the label by its critics as "the bottle-scarred community."

My beat included whatever was happening in the north of England—murders, bombings, holdups, human interest stories, potholers trapped in caves, climbers dying on mountains, airliner and train crashes. In short, I covered anything and everything, the articles ranging in length from one paragraph to several columns. I grew to love the earthiness of the Lancashire and Yorkshire people and their dialects. Once I was trying to interview a most reluctant Liverpool woman who kept shouting at me: "Sling yer 'ook! Sling yer 'ook!" From the strident tone I interpreted the phrase to mean I should hastily depart, which I did. Afterwards I inquired as to its origin. The term derives from the orders a captain would give to a seaman whom he was dismissing to unhook his hammock from its sling and quit the ship.

When asking directions to a place, Lancashire people would say, "Turn left at the robots." These, I discovered, were traffic lights. When people said they were "starved," it did not mean they were hungry but were cold. If a southerner like me stood at the bar of a public house deep in that country it would be impossible to understand anything being said, so thick were their dialects and use of idiom. But when they addressed me, these gracious, warmhearted northerners politely modified their speech and were quite understandable.

Coming into the office at lunchtime one Sunday in 1954, I was told that the theater correspondent was absent—therefore I was to go and interview Vivien Leigh, who was opening a new play at a Manchester theater prior to its London opening. This was completely off my beat; what was I to ask her? You'll think of something, came the news editor's answer. I spent the afternoon watching a full dress rehearsal of Terence Rattigan's new play *Separate Tables* and marveled at just how beautiful Ms. Leigh looked onstage, unchanged from her great Hollywood stardom days in *Gone with the Wind* and *A Streetcar Named Desire*. In the theater, Laurence Olivier graciously introduced me to the cast, director, and the famous London theatrical producer Binkie Beaumont. Then we repaired to the Midland Hotel where Ms. Leigh changed and came down to meet me in a room off the main lounge. It was a disappointing surprise to see her up close, across a coffee table, for her face was an unattractive mass of tiny wrinkles, presumably from smoking. As I struggled through my unprepared interview, I was somewhat disconcerted that Olivier stood close by and monitored every word exchanged between us. I did not learn why until a few months later when I read that at around this time Ms. Leigh was having a love affair with the Australian actor Peter Finch. Olivier was ready to pounce if the affair or anything else he didn't like came up, but, not being in the West End gossip circle, I was ignorant. After the interview, the couple got into their Rolls Royce, and Olivier drove off. Due to her busy schedule, Ms. Leigh did not open the play in London. Dogged all her life with bipolar disease, Ms. Leigh died of tuberculosis in 1967 at age fifty-four.

My reporting days at the *Daily Mail* were notable for one big story that was entirely and deliberately falsified and two scoops, one of which was true and the other of which was accidentally untrue. The three tales illustrate the strange nature of journalism.

Throughout the 1950s and 1960s—in Britain—there was a hugely popular radio soap opera called *The Archers: An Everyday Story of Country Life*. It was broadcast every evening between 6:30 and 7:00 p.m. As happens in long-running shows, one of the actresses wanted to leave. So in one night's episode, the actress playing Grace Archer in the story went into a barn that caught afire and was trapped by a wind-slammed door.

The "death" of this much-loved and admired character stunned millions of listeners. Why did she have to die? My ineffable editor Howard French heard complaints and arguments about Grace's departure at a dinner party that night and at 11 p.m. he flounced into the editorial room and told Jimmy Lewthwaite that he wanted a public opinion quiz done immediately. By this, he meant the then fashionable journalistic technique of going out into the street and interviewing random passersby for their opinions on the issue of the day. A little picture accompanied the instant pearls of wisdom that the pedestrians were asked to come up with.

Jimmy ordered a photographer and me to go out at once. At about 11:15 p.m. we hit the streets of downtown Manchester looking for interviewees. Because it was a cold winter's night, there were none. We paced up and down the main thoroughfares looking for customers, but there was not even a drunk to be seen. At 11:30 p.m., we rushed back and reported to Jimmy that we had nothing. "Call the ambulance and fire stations and ask their staffs for opinions," he barked. I did. But not one person would admit to having heard the radio show. At 11:45 p.m., I again told Jimmy that I was empty-handed. "And you know, I'm good at these quizzes," I said.

Jimmy pondered for a moment. During the previous week, Mr. French had fired one reporter for not writing as good a story as a rival at the *Daily Express* and two subeditors (copyeditors) whose work was not up to his standards.

"If we don't have a story within fifteen minutes we'll probably both lose our jobs," said Jimmy, who was nearing retirement. "Go out and write the entire story."

"You mean . . . from imagination?"

"Do what you have to do, Derek."

So, thinking of my wife and small children, the fight it had required to get onto a national newspaper, and the poor prospects for future employment were I to be fired, I invented the entire story. I dreamed up realistic-sounding statements from people I assigned to live in roads that I knew were several miles long. It was not our policy to give house numbers, thus people could not question whether my imaginary interviewees were real neighbors. I had plumbers and carpenters giving feisty views about the ethics of Grace's untimely death, while housewives lamented that they would never hear her dulcet tones again.

Jimmy ran his eagle eye over the story quickly and rushed it to the editorial production department in the nick of time. An hour later my article, dominating half a page, was on the streets. I even got a "Thank you for a good effort" note from Mr. French. The complete untruthfulness of the article did not bother me because I was inventing opinions about a purely fictitious character and what had happened to her on radio "soap." If Grace Archer had been a real person, I would have admitted failure to find interviewees and taken the consequences. Jimmy Lewthwaite felt the same: why should we lose our jobs because the crazy Mr. French wanted opinions on a nonevent?

The other scoop I secured that also turned out to be almost totally inaccurate illustrates the pressures of instant journalism. In the bars around the *Daily Mail* office the incident became jocularly known as "The day Humphry killed six lions single-handedly." The story began when the Manchester Fire Brigade reported to us at 3 a.m. that they had been called to the then world-famous Belle Vue Zoo, where the offices and animal buildings were well afire. Because our last edition printed at 4 a.m., I was rushed off to the zoo with orders to telephone in a fast report by 3:30 a.m. Within ten minutes, I arrived and saw a Noah's Ark scene of elephants, zebras, goats, and giraffes being led or herded through the zoo's gardens and down the lamp-lit city streets to safety. It was an eerie sight, but there was no photographer there to record it. Belle Vue was famed for its collection of lions, so I quickly made for their quarters. How could these difficult animals be controlled or be rescued in the middle of such an inferno? Flames were licking ominously through the rafters of the all-wooden lion house. The chief custodian, armed with a large boar hunting rifle, was standing ready to shoot as the frightened beasts cowered in the corner furthest from the inferno.

"What are you going to do?" I asked him.

"There's no way we can remove them safely on such short notice," he replied. "I shall shoot them all in minute."

My deadline was dangerously close. I raced out of the zoo into the street to find a telephone. As I ran, shots rang out, and I carefully counted seven—the number of lions the zoo owned. With barely seconds to spare I dictated my story, reporting that the illustrious lions had all been executed to prevent their being burned to death or escaping.

Whatever happened to the zoo now was of no importance to me because there were no more editions that night. I strolled back across the zoo's grounds just to observe what was developing. Halfway back I met the lion custodian still holding his rifle.

"That must have been terrible for you," I said sympathetically.

"No, it wasn't too bad," he replied. "It took me seven shots to kill the first animal, and by then the firemen said that they had the blaze under control. So the rest were saved."

I was pleased for the safety of the six lions, of course, but horrified at the possible consequences of my story. What a gaffe! A glance at my watch showed that the paper was already printing. There was nothing I could now do to correct my blunder. I decided to keep quiet, brazen it out, and see what happened. I could well be fired.

When I reached the office the next day nothing was said by anybody, but my "in-box" contained a note from the editor. He complimented me on the zoo blaze story, which no other newspaper had even mentioned, and enclosed a check for twenty-five pounds as a bonus.

HELPING RUSSIA

My outstanding scoop while reporting for the *Daily Mail* (and sometimes moonlighting on its weekend edition, the *Sunday Dispatch*, to earn a little extra money) was connected to Sputnik 1, the first space satellite put into orbit in October 1957. The Russian achievement had astonished the world, not least the American government who had not thought that the competition was so technologically advanced. Writing of the event twenty-five years later, Hugh Sidey said in *Time* magazine (January 12, 1981): "Power and politics were never the same again. . . Sputnik One signaled a new super-power on the prowl."

After only a few days, the Russian astronomers lost track of their satellite. That circumstance—aided by fog—enabled me to get my scoop. Every evening that week, along with other reporters, I had traveled to Jodrell Bank Observatory, in a village some forty miles from Manchester. This was the site of the world's first radio telescope for research of the moon and the stars. This creation of the brilliant British astronomer, Bernard Lovell, professor of radio astronomy at Manchester University, although partly constructed from leftover World War II parts, cost the British government several million dollars. The 250-foot revolving parabolic bowl, weighing over two thousand tons, was a scientific and engineering marvel in the 1950s. Up until then, looking at the sky and outer space was done visually through telescopes; Lovell pioneered looking at space via radio signals, a development of the radar system he had helped construct during the war. Since the launching of Sputnik 1, journalists like me had been trekking daily to Jodrell Bank hoping Professor Lovell would have something to tell us about it. He was the only available man in the free world who could track what was happening; he also had a flair for interpreting to it to nonscientists.

The early visits that week were all fruitless, and my enthusiasm had waned. Still, it was a quiet Saturday evening, so Jimmy Lewthwaite told me to drive out to Jodrell Bank to check up. On the way I ran into dense fog, making it impossible to see more than a few feet. What little traffic there was on the road ground to a halt. Drivers abandoned their cars and started to walk home. The difference between my not being able to drive at all and moving along at a snail's pace was the ability to see through the wet windshield. I could not safely move at all—but, fortunately, my old Ford Eight had a crude windshield that folded up to allow fresh air through in hot weather. So, with poor but accurate vision, and feeling very cold, I was able to drive at a walking pace through the thickest banks of fog. I reached Jodrell Bank at roughly 9 p.m. No other reporters arrived, presumably turned back by the fog.

Professor Lovell was an affable man who relied upon the presence of the press since he was meeting huge governmental and parliamentary criticism for overspending on the construction of his radio telescope. His first blueprint called for an open mesh dish (unlike today's domestic, dinner-plate-style television satellite dishes), but he had decided that the instrument would be more effective if it were filled in with panels. He installed the paneling, nearly doubling the cost, without asking government permission and was now in a heap of political trouble.

"Do you have anything for me tonight?" I asked Professor Lovell.

"Yes, the Astronomical Council in Moscow has officially asked me to help them find Sputnik 1," he replied. "They seem to have lost track of it."

Imagine my delight! I telephoned Jimmy to tell him of the coming story. Lovell had received a telegram from Moscow via the ordinary post office telegraph system telling him where Sputnik had last been seen and where they thought it might be next. This was quite a turnabout. When Sputnik was first launched, Lovell had asked Russia officials for information so that he could cooperate in tracking it but had met with Cold War–style silence. From observations he had been taking during the week, Lovell knew the Russians were hopelessly wrong in their calculations. Now they were fishing for information, both about where the satellite was and also about his instrument's ability to track it. Lovell told me that he would be unable to get a fix on Sputnik until about 10 p.m., when it would probably be in an azimuth where his radio telescope could locate it.

The following is how I described it in next morning's *Sunday Dispatch*:

> I was standing behind Professor Lovell and his team in the Jodrell Bank "moon house" when the rocket was sighted. It showed as a series of noisy zigzags on a screen like the normal household TV set. As the screen crackled with life, showing up a radar impression of the 18,000 mph rocket, cameras whirled, recording its invaluable data. The rocket is now 80 minutes ahead of the earth satellite. It only needs to gain another 16 minutes to catch and pass the satellite in orbit.

Professor Lovell wrote a telegram to the astronomers in Moscow telling them exactly where in space their equipment was flying. He then basked in the limelight of his achievement. Scientifically, what he had done was well within the scope of his telescope, no more than a bit of practice for his staff. But the canny Lovell, who was under political pressure about his overspending, played the publicity for all it was worth. He gave me a statement:

"We are demonstrating the tremendous power of the radio tele-scope to the Russians and the whole of the world."

My story made the front-page splash headlines in next day's paper. Regardless of whether it illustrated Britain's technologi-cal prowess, the Russian event got Lovell off the hook, and I was a happy young reporter. Passing by Jodrell Bank recently, I saw a veritable sea of massive radio telescopes. The original one is still in use fifty years later, linked to many others in a world network searching the cosmos.

Nuclear Baptism

I was reminded of what could be called a "baptism by nuclear fire" in my own career when the awful Chernobyl nuclear disas-ter happened in Russia in 1986. In 1957, the editor asked me to become assistant night news editor to Jimmy Lewthwaite. This meant working even closer with my revered mentor as well as a much-needed salary increase to twenty-three pounds a week. I had been reporting for the *Daily Mail* for two fascinating years; at twenty-seven I was taking my first little step on the promotion ladder.

On October 7, 1957, Jimmy took the night off from work, and I was put in charge of the news-gathering for northern England. The day news editor left at 6 p.m. when all was quiet, and I took over. It being a Friday night, I anticipated a gentle introduction to my new role, which I needed because almost all the reporters were older and far more experienced.

It turned out to be the night of the world's first nuclear power station disaster—right in my bailiwick!

At the news desk, we began to get vague reports of some-thing sinister happening at the Windscale plutonium production plant in Cumberland. Fire brigades all over the north of England were alerted, and a few had set out already for Windscale. As a reporter, I had made two visits to the nuclear plant during the previous year. I had actually stood with others on the nuclear core looking down through the immense glass shield at the plutonium rods. Although I had no scientific training, my visits to Windscale had given me a sound briefing of the type, scale, and danger of the work going on there.

I soon realized that a major accident had occurred, although the police chiefs were trying to allay panic by saying that it was a small incident, already under control. Every reporter on the staff was put onto the story, telephoning or doing research. It was a cardinal rule of the newspaper that as soon as there was a hint of a big story, reporters must be dispatched to the scene immediately, even if it proved to be a false alarm. Better to be there first—and mistaken—than not to have gone at all. The atomic plant was remotely situated on the Cumberland coast some two hundred miles from Manchester; it was slightly closer to Liverpool and Newcastle, where we had reporters stationed.

I telephoned Liverpool and Newcastle and asked them to set out for Windscale. They refused to go! Having read about the atomic bombs dropped on Hiroshima and Nagasaki in 1945, they were not ignorant of the dangers of nuclear fallout. They informed me bluntly that they put their own lives before their jobs.

"Go partway, telephone me, and then we'll make a fresh assessment of the danger," I coaxed. They would not budge.

So on my first night in command, I had a rebellion on my hands—of course, one with which I sympathized. I realized it was best to break the house rule and not send out anyone on this most unusual story that included the risk of contamination. Instead, we pulled out the telephone directories and began telephoning every inhabitant in the surrounding area. Gradually, we pieced together the best story that was available that night.

Over the following weeks and months, it emerged that a fire in the reactor's nuclear core had caused a cloud of radioactive gas to be released from a 405-foot high chimney stack. Extensive fallout had drifted across the English countryside. Farm vegetables and milk production within two hundred square miles were banned from sale, while many cows and sheep thought to be contaminated were slaughtered.

The National Radiological Protection Board of England has estimated that the accident caused as many as thirty-three subsequent cancer deaths by humans. So, we were quite correct in not going near this particular story in person. And I survived in my new job, able to fight again another day.

During these years, I never wanted to be a foreign correspondent because the long absences the assignments entail would interfere with my family life. Spending time with Jean and the three boys was of paramount importance to me after the ragtag way that I had grown up. From around ten years old, Edgar and Clive became enthusiastic racing cyclists, so I had the pleasure of driving them around the southeast of England to race meetings or velodromes. Powerfully built Edgar was particularly good at certain distances and won several distinctions; people said he could have a future in professional cycling, but after early enthusiasm for the idea he lost interest. Clive's interest dropped for several years, but then, in his thirties, he took up amateur cycling again with determination, competing in time trials and hill climbs. Now in his fifties, in France where he now lives, he rides with a club usually twice a week. Stephen was never interested in cycling—fishing was his sport, and later also golf.

None of the boys wanted to follow me into journalism and I never pressed them to do so. After office jobs in the city of

London, Edgar and Clive realized they wanted to be their own bosses and started looking around for entrepreneurial opportunities. A friend showed them how to profitably recycle broken automobile transmissions (known as "gearboxes" in Britain). Soon they were doing good business in this line for the next twenty or so years. After several office jobs, Stephen settled down to permanent employment with a heating and cooling company. As with so many young people today, Stephen never married, Edgar was married briefly, while Clive in contrast has been married for more than twenty-five years, with two grown children.

Chapter 7

WORLD'S GREATEST PAPER

I N 1967, I WAS fortunate enough to land a job on what was
then the world's greatest newspaper, the *Sunday Times* of London. Between about 1960 and 1980 this journal was recognized
worldwide as the highest quality newspaper anywhere, with its
scoops, pioneering investigative journalism (the Insight team),
thoughtful coverage of books and the arts, and trendy style and
fashion reporting. (It still is a good newspaper but lacks the
thrust, blunt commentary, and pizzazz that the earlier paper had
in abundance.) With a circulation of over a million, its writers
won many prizes and even had songs written about it. Everybody
who was anybody read the *Sunday Times*, if for no other reason
than to keep abreast of swinging London. It was the first newspaper to have a color magazine. Through huge advertising revenues, it was also extremely prosperous for its then-owner, the
Canadian businessman Roy Thomson, and he sensibly plowed
a lot of this revenue back into the editorial budget. The editor could spend what and how he liked—but only up to a point
fixed by Thomson, which was rumored to be around one million

pounds a year. Shrewdly, the editors, first Denis Hamilton and then the mercurial Harold Evans, made it their top priority to recruit journalists, artists, cartoonists, photographers, and designers of real talent and originality. They were carefree and pleasantly mad, many of them, but were brilliant people who turned in journalism of quality when needed. Although I had already been in journalism for twenty-one years, working on five newspapers, I realized that I had stepped into an absolutely fresh, action-driven, superior world of words when I joined the staff.

I reached the *Sunday Times* in a roundabout way. After five years on the *Daily Mail*, I wanted a more challenging job. Television's spurt in growth in the early 1960s was affecting newspapers by filching staff, affecting advertising revenues, and, more importantly, taking away the exclusive dependence the public had on newspapers for their news, sports results, and entertainment. I decided that I wanted to edit a regional newspaper—to be a big fish in a little pond and to run my own newspaper. So in 1960 I joined Home Counties Newspapers, in Luton, Bedfordshire, for the reason that they owned a chain of around twenty local newspapers. I became deputy editor of the *Luton News* with a promise of an editorship when a vacancy arose. This occurred in 1963 when I took over the editorship of the *Romford Recorder*, later renamed the *Havering Recorder*. It was a bright tabloid weekly with fierce competition coming from the *Romford Times*. This area of London is to the east of the Cockney world of Bethnal Green, and many of its inhabitants work for the Ford Motor Company, which has been in Romford since the 1920s.

I had a staff of ten reporters and four copyeditors, almost all young and inexperienced. On top of that, the staff was always revolving. As soon as I had trained a new journalist, he or she would be recruited to a Fleet Street newspaper to replace staff that had moved to television. My youngsters could take these more glamorous jobs without leaving home, Fleet Street being an easy thirty-minute train commute. Despite this staffing frustration, I enjoyed the job of turning out a smart, newsy issue every Thursday night. For two years it was rewarding, but then things started to unravel. When you are a big fish in a little pond, you have to cope with other fish that are narrow-minded and irritating. There were petty disagreements over language, arguments over who was really in charge of the editorial content of the newspaper, and turmoil over the dismal company policy of promoting staff only by length of service. I wanted merit promotions; the company would not budge. In the end, the directors and I were so severely in disagreement that it was mutually agreed that I would leave, taking a nice compensation package with me.

What to do next? Fortune shone on me. At that very point the prestigious and prosperous *Sunday Times* bought the daily *Times*, which was in financial trouble. It was intended to leave the daily newspaper to carry on as before, but the deputy editor of the Sunday paper, William Rees-Mogg, became its new editor and took a few key staff with him, leaving openings on the Sunday paper. The managing editor of the Sunday version now became editor. This was Harold Evans, a hard-charging, creative journalist who specialized in newspaper design. Although he inherited a host of talent and a journal with a huge reputation for quality, he soon began to shake the paper up in many ways. For one thing, he wanted even more scoops. It seems that when he looked at the reporting staff, he saw too many people with university, upper-class backgrounds—a bunch of good men and women, but lacking in "foot-in-the-door" type of aggressive reporting skills. I had known Harry when we both worked on the *Manchester Evening News* in the 1950s. Currently, I was doing part-time work for the *Daily Mail*, waiting for a vacancy so that

I could rejoin it. The *Evening Standard* offered me a job but as a copyeditor, which I didn't really want to be. I yearned to go back to reporting. The great newspaper in Chancery Lane (not in Fleet Street where I had started) beckoned, and I wrote to Harry for a job—and immediately got it. At the same time he recruited people like John Ball, crime reporter of the *Daily Express*, and Anne Robinson, a tough journalist with news agency and *Daily Mail* experience, who went on to have a distinguished career with other newspapers and in international television (notably *Watchdog* and the *Weakest Link*).

Although recruited as a reporter, I was asked to become the paper's letters editor temporarily, as the present one was leaving for an editorship of a provincial newspaper. Being the editor of the letters-to-the-editor page of a world-renowned journal was an unusual job. I started work on a Wednesday to assess the readership's response to the news, views, and arts coverage of the previous Sunday, usually around two hundred letters. This job had the benefit of quickly enabling me to know the entire editorial staff of just over one hundred talents, because it was the policy that every incoming letter must be shown to the writer who was being praised or criticized. In a quiet, personal way I soon came to know and understand the array of talented writers that the paper had assembled. I had to assess his or her response to the letters, and a reply had to be written, or perhaps the letter printed on Sunday. I made the initial choice of the letters to be printed and laid out the letters page, while Chief Editor Harold Evans supervised my selection closely just as he scrupulously oversaw the tone of the whole paper.

It soon became obvious to me that it is the readers who hate what an article says who are stirred to write a critical letter to the editor. Those who agree with an article are unlikely to do anything. Why bother to praise it? Sometimes the paper would get dozens of letters hammering an article for what people claimed was wrong with it—perhaps for what they saw as its lack of balance or what it had failed to say. (At the height of its campaigning era, the *Sunday Times* sometimes received up to ten libel writs, or threats of writs, in a week, which I of course instantly passed over to the legal department.) As I have previously mentioned in my earlier accounts of my *Manchester Evening News* and *Daily Mail* days, newspapers resort not infrequently to inventive journalism. The *Sunday Times* sometimes came close to that subterfuge also. When an extraordinary volume of letters attacked a specific article, making it look as though the article was terribly wrong when actually it was not, Harold Evans would ask me to telephone a few people and suggest that they might contribute a supportive letter—hastily taken down over the telephone on a Friday. No letter printed in the paper was ever invented, but they were sometimes solicited in order to present a balanced view.

After a year as letters editor, I returned to the newsroom as a reporter, which was what I had come for. No longer did I yearn to climb to executive positions. Investigating and writing were what I wanted to do. Later on when I was offered the job of news editor, I instinctively turned it down. But it wasn't long before I was taken off the news staff again. In the late sixties, England, like the US, was going through considerable racial unrest. The spokesman for the white point of view was Conservative Member of Parliament Enoch Powell, a highly intelligent demagogue. I listened to him speak many times; it was always notable that the audience appeared to hang on every word, even though they may not have agreed with all of it. Powell, who in a previous government had been minister for health, led a campaign to have all black immigrants returned to their original countries. The Conservative Party of the day, under Edward Heath, to its credit would have nothing to do with the racist send-them-back campaign and excommunicated Powell from its ranks.

In one startling speech, Powell, who had been a classical scholar and spoke several languages, used a metaphor to predict that there would soon be violence between England's black and white populations. "I see the river Tiber flowing with blood," he told an audience, hiding behind the words of the Roman poet Virgil. He was shrewd enough to dodge anti-discrimination laws by quoting an ancient poet instead of himself predicting violence. But everybody knew what he meant. The speech shocked the nation. There were many who agreed with Powell, but huge numbers were appalled that Britain had come to such intolerance. It seemed the nation that had not long ago run the largest empire in the world, including millions of people of color in Africa, the West Indies, and India, was now disowning them when they were living nearby.

Almost all the black population of Britain had come in after 1950 to fill the jobs that English people would not do. In most cases, the London government had gone out to its former colonies—the West Indies, India, Pakistan, Bangladesh, and a few others—to actively recruit people to come to work in Britain. They were needed to sweep the streets, collect the trash, clean the hospitals, and so forth. The white population had become economically better off and spurned such work. Unlike many other European countries, the British said that the immigrants could bring their entire families once they had settled in. Up until 1950, Britain had been a homogenous society, with people of color only seen in shipping ports. Powell and his supporters did not like strangers from other lands pouring in with their children, parents, and even grandparents. They resented the way immigrants spoke differently, dressed in another way—even the new smells of their cooking cuisine became focuses of resentment.

Through polling and demonstrations, it became apparent that millions supported Powell's send-them-back campaign. The slogan "Enoch was right" was painted on hundreds of walls.

Immediately after Powell's notorious "rivers of blood" speech, the *Sunday Times*—alone—published a scathing editorial opinion article calling him in no uncertain terms "a racist." Just as quickly, Powell sued for libel. The only defense to a libel accusation in Britain is justification that what was printed was true. It looked to be the libel action of the century—the spokesman for the bigots versus the gutsy newspaper of the liberal left. (In political and social policy, the paper declared itself "independent," but its style and opinions were invariably left of center.) Not accustomed to backing down on anything, and possessing the financial strength to cope with the potential enormous expenses of the case, the legal advisors and the editorial chiefs decided to defend the lawsuit. They set out to prove that Powell was a racist and was causing unrest in the country.

I was surprised to be called into an editorial/legal conference and asked to leave the newsroom temporarily and become an investigator for the legal department. My brief was to tour the country, regardless of expense, to gather firsthand accounts of how black people had been treated by whites whenever Powell spoke. This would be the paper's justification for the alleged libel. Every Friday evening for the next six months I returned to the office and typed up my reports, handing them to the legal department, not the news editor.

This unusual assignment inevitably led me to become friends with scores of people in the black communities. I usually started with a meeting with leaders—Muslim, Sikh, Hindu, gospel churches, and occasionally Black Panthers. They would point out to me the ordinary folk who they had heard were the victims of racial slurs and abuse. For example, some people related arriving at work after a Powell speech and seeing wall slogans such as "Powell is right" and "Go Home Pakis." Others gave me evidence of how they had not gained, or lost a job, or were not able to find a home, because of the racial hatred stirred up by Powell. This was exactly the evidence we were seeking for the court case. Naturally I learned a lot about the customs and habits of the many races of people now living in Britain and built friendships that existed long afterwards. When incidents that appeared to have a racial undertone broke out over the following years, I was able to enter and move around the "ghettos" freely when other journalists were ordered out. More than an investigative reporter, I had now also become the paper's race relations correspondent. I kept a large, detailed address book of everybody I had met during the Powell inquiry, and this was a gold mine for the next ten years.

Six months after the writ was issued, Powell dropped his libel action. Each side paid their own costs. There were two reasons: first, the mountain of information connecting Powell to racial hatred that I had collected, and second, the *Sunday Times* demanded, and a court agreed, that Powell must hand over the letters from his constituents whom he had quoted publicly saying demeaning things about colored immigrants. This Powell would not do.

While this first period of racial turmoil in Britain lasted, several academics and social psychologists published books analyzing the problem. I bought them all. Very few other people did—particularly not the people in the workplace and communities where better understanding of racial differences would have been helpful. The books contained many academic jargon terms that I had difficulty interpreting. From this came my idea to write a book that explained black people to white people, their customs, mores, and problems. It would be in crisp language, with no difficult words or jargon. Small, cheap, and paperback. To help me explain the black predicament of immigrants from the Caribbean, I drew in as coauthor a social worker born in Antigua, Gus John, who had gone undercover in the Handsworth ghetto, Birmingham, for six months to investigate the conditions of immigrants there. Gus knew firsthand what was happening—and he could write. I had all the background and stories from the Powell investigation, which the *Sunday Times* agreed I could use. (This was its policy for all staff, on the grounds that the paper benefited from the reflected glory of the books. When he was on the staff of the paper, Ian Fleming began his James Bond books; over the years, many staffers produced remarkable books.)

As we were finishing the book, while I was pondering a good title, I heard a BBC reporter on the radio ask a West Indian woman why she and others could not get housing. She shouted back: "Because they're black!" Immediately, I knew that that terse, sharp phrase was the title of the book. Penguin Books had a special division for controversial, original paperbacks, and they published ours in 1972. It sold moderately well, receiving thoughtful reviews. Penguin were dithering about whether to print more when out of the blue came an announcement that *Because They're Black* had won the Martin Luther King Memorial Prize for that year as the book published in America or Britain most likely to improve race relations. This was the era when the assassination of MLK in 1968 was deeply troubling to all people concerned with racial equality. (It still is, of course, but in the five years immediately after his murder it was an especially raw point.) The prize money of one hundred pounds (about two hundred dollars) was put up by an Anglo-American science-fiction writer, John Brunner, for many years. (The prize seems not to exist any longer.) But as the award drew attention back to our book, Penguin was soon issuing another edition, and sales were brisk. Gus John and I donated the prize money to a youth hostel in Moss Side, Manchester. Did the book achieve its aim of getting white workers to better understand their black counterparts? Impossible to know. But it might have helped a bit.

For the next few years, I wrote bylined stories for the paper as well as ones about immigration and race. I was never a front-page scoop writer because I did not work in the fields of politics and war. I was essentially an inside-page reporter. Mostly working alone, my forte was the investigation of what lay behind the big story of that week. Why had the explosion happened? Which criminal gang was behind the raid? Who was pulling the strings of a racket? My tactics were to quietly gather background during the week, rarely speaking at press conferences so as not to give away to the reporters' "pack" what line I was taking. When an ordinary member of the public finds himself or herself suddenly in the news, they usually clam up, both out of nervousness and from not completely understanding what has happened. They might also be aggrieved at any misreporting in the haste of first reporting. In these cases I would wait until Friday night or Saturday morning before approaching the key people, quietly tell them who I was, and offer to publish a definitive explanation of why the event had happened.

The managing editor of news, Michael Randall, a former editor of the *Daily Mail* and a competent and likeable man, knew how to use his staff according to not only their talents but their predilections. I disliked politics, war, show business, and fluffy stories. Thus, I became the reporter assigned to what is called in the profession "shit subjects" as well as race and immigration matters. Probably the most morbid of them all was about a resurgence of scrotal cancer. Nobody else in the newsroom wanted to inquire into what lay behind a brief article in an abstruse medical journal concerning the upsurge in a deadly cancer of the testicles in certain factory workers. But my eventual series of articles brought about not only medical and public awareness but official reforms that undoubtedly saved lives.

The deadly cancer of the scrotum was fairly well known in Victorian times because little orphanage boys who swept the chimneys of rich people frequently died of it. Clambering up through the soot and scraping it away so the chimney worked better resulted in their being covered in soot, which is largely made up of mineral oil. On most of the human body mineral oil has little effect, but on the scrotum it rapidly develops into cancer. Unknown hundreds of chimney sweep boys died in agony of the disease, as well as suffering burns and deformed joints. Charles Kingsley was the first to expose the scandal is his famous book *The Water Babies*, published in 1863. As chimneys became smaller, and more efficient methods of cleaning them developed, thankfully the boy chimney sweeps were no longer needed. This particular form of cancer became almost unknown. Doctors were no longer trained to detect and treat it—which was unfortunate, because if treated immediately it is completely curable. Moreover, if a person comes into contact with this carcinogenic substance, scrupulous instant cleanliness prevents disease. Unnoticed until my news editor spotted a mention in a remote journal, the disease had reared its ugly head again in modern industry.

As heavy industry grew more sophisticated after World War II, different mineral oils were needed to lubricate and cool fast machinery. Some may have been even more carcinogenic. Most at risk were the tool setters as they straddled the equipment to maintain it. The dangerous oils splashed onto their groin areas; sometimes they put oily rags in their pockets, then left the factory without changing or showering, doing so after cycling home. Even the cycling added to the problem of infection. Little did these men know what was happening because the cancer might not develop for seven or even seventy years. Some were by then working in other jobs or retired. Some were too embarrassed to report the painless white warts on their testicles until the cancer had reached a fatal stage. Often the treating doctor did not know what the symptoms were until it was too late. Thus, hundreds of British workers were dying of an avoidable cancer. In 1968 and 1969, I published in the *Sunday Times* a series of four articles on the scandal of "The cancer that is spread by shyness," driving home the point that good hygiene was the first answer, purer oils the second, and that medical education should be improved. Nobody had talked openly about this disease for years, but lawsuits from widows were beginning to appear in the courts. As a result of my articles, questions were asked in the House of Commons urging the government to introduce screening for the disease and forcing factories and plants to provide better protective clothing and mandating on-the-spot personal hygiene. Government rules followed, enforcing superior cleanliness and routine testing—no longer could any worker go home without these precautions.

My campaign came too late to save those workers already at risk, but it almost certainly saved many lives in the future. Campaigning journalism has some rewards, largely unseen.

The *Sunday Times* was wealthy enough to have sufficient staff to allow them to stay with a running story, or a campaign, for months. For me, this was the case throughout 1969 when there was a huge anti-apartheid campaign to stop the South African national cricket team from playing in England. Led by a twenty-year-old student, Peter Hain, the protesters pulled every move in the civil disobedience book of tricks to embarrass the English and South African authorities to call off the tour. Gluing up hotel door locks, throwing flour bombs, running on the pitches at crucial moments during play, distracting players from the stands, staging sit-down strikes in vital places, and digging up key parts of the pitches in the night were all part of the campaign. Taking his cue from Mahatma Gandhi and Martin Luther King, Hain and colleagues stuck to purely nonviolent methods. They were frequently arrested by police for "disturbing the peace" and "conspiracy" to disrupt public functions.

Over the two years in which I reported this fascinating campaign—the first such in Britain—I broke another standard of journalistic ethics by becoming a friend of Peter and his family. It was inevitable. His parents, Adeline and Walter, were charming people with liberal politics and an ever-open house. And I needed the inside track on the campaign. The Hains had exiled themselves from their homeland, South Africa, after a public row over the funeral of a friend. Mr. Hain Sr. was scheduled to read the funeral oration, but the government issued an order banning him from doing this. Without hesitation, his eleven-year-old son Peter stepped forward and read it instead. A resolute campaigner was born.

It wasn't Hain's group alone that protested. Many bishops and Members of Parliament argued forcefully that it was an offense to Britain's racial minority to have players from an apartheid country using its hallowed cricket pitches. It was a national debate. The South African cricket tour was canceled. Hain's Stop-The-Seventy-Tour campaign was credited or blamed, depending on one's view of politics and the sanctity of cricket, the national game. I published a little book about it, mainly from trial reports, called *The Cricket Conspiracy*, which had little impact because the whole campaign was over and forgotten by the time it appeared.

Our friendship faded when I moved to America not long after. He entered politics, first as a member of parliament, and later as a government, then cabinet, minister, when the Labor Party won the 1995 election. I almost fell off my chair one day when reading in a newspaper that Peter had been appointed the UK's "minister for Africa." What an irony after his early life! Later he became minister for Europe and minister for Northern Ireland.

I had a strange relationship with the fascists in Britain. The British National Party (BNP) made black immigrants their main target for vicious hatred and sometimes violence. Enoch Powell was their saint. Although I was the best-known race relations reporter in the country, and by constant association in print must, inevitably, have shown my sympathies, I could always have a relaxed interview with the BNP leadership. They knew I was against what they stood for, but they also trusted that I would not misrepresent or vilify them. This was never more borne out when the American white supremacist and KKK leader from Louisiana, David Duke, planned to come to London to speak to his fellow racists. The British Government issued an order banning him from entry. Despite that, newspapers were saying that he had already entered by a back door, probably via Ireland. But no newsmen or police could find him. At my desk on Saturday morning, March 4, 1978, my phone rang.

"This is David Duke. Do you want to come and interview me?"

We arranged a meeting place in a car park. My cameraman colleague snapped him as we talked. Nothing he said was of much interest to a liberal-left paper like mine, so the next day we casually reported that Duke was in town, that we'd seen him, and that was that. He quickly disappeared back to America.

The leadership of the black community became angry with me when I reported in a big *Sunday Times* article that muggings of people in London and Birmingham had increased dramatically. Almost entirely to blame were gangs of black youths who had come to the country as babies when their parents sought work. Now teenagers, they were poorly educated, jobless, drifting, and dumped in an affluent white world that cared nothing about them. Inevitably they turned to crime to survive. My article troubled editor Harold Evans so much that he held it back for three weeks and went over its facts and statements meticulously, until eventually agreeing to publish. Evans was extremely sensitive to racial problems and feared being blamed for causing unrest. I told him: "It's the truth of what's happening on our streets at night. Both black and white residents are furious about these crimes, afraid to walk the streets. If we publish, perhaps something will get done about it."

After it appeared in the newspaper, I was flooded with praise from those who recognized the need to address the problem; others boasted, "We told you so, Powell was right." My friends in the black community initially were shocked and angry that I had exposed this running sore in their world. Yet, when they saw the impact of the article on television and radio, along with worldwide syndication in print, and how it had started a meaningful dialogue about how to better look after these lost teenagers, particularly their education and job opportunities, they tempered their criticisms and did their best to resolve it. Over the next few years, the level of muggings in the cities considerably diminished.

Over my twelve years at the *Sunday Times*, my scrapbooks show that I wrote about dozens of subjects other than race: rows over porn literature, police violence and corruption, the Northern Ireland civil war, prison standards, wrongful imprisonments, and so on, but mostly about civil liberties issues. The paper devised an intelligent system to cover the killing war in Ulster as most newspapers were finding that journalists based too long in that troubled and dangerous area were apt to lose their professional and emotional balance. My paper's way to keep the coverage high quality and the staff on an even keel was to assign a team of ten reporters, male and female, to rotate two or three at a time, depending on the newsworthiness of events there. Even if you were not in the province, you had to keep yourself abreast of events there so that when you returned you were up to speed already. And you knew you could not be there longer than two weeks. This roster system worked well; I went in and out of Northern Ireland for ten years. The strain of covering a civil war in one's own backyard could be seen even at the dinner table in our hotel when journalists were supposed to relax. Reporters and photographers would keep repeating over and over the horrible things, the remarkable demonstrations, that they had witnessed that day. This obsession became so disturbing that I instituted a personal rule immediately after we took our places at dinner: "No war! Save your stories for the paper." As I was usually the senior journalist present—and it was commonsense anyway—my pronouncement was accepted. We relaxed for a while.

Like all journalists covering the Irish troubles, I had my share of near misses with regard to hotel bombings, chiefly at the Europa Hotel in Belfast, and getting doses of tear gas when watching a demonstration. If rubber bullets were being fired by the British Army, one learned to drop into a crouching position, turning sideways, so as to protect the stomach and chest. In contrast to the war in Iraq, I don't recall any journalist being killed. The targets were government buildings and British soldiers. Yet I did have two scary events. On one of my early visits I was walking down a Belfast street when I felt a gun being stuck in my back. "Keep walking," a man's voice right behind me said. It was like something out of a gangster film. Then: "Go into the next doorway." I was pushed up against a wall and frisked. After I explained who I was and showed him my National Union of

Journalists identity card, the man said: "We were just checking who was in the area," and he disappeared.

My other run-in with the IRA was more stressful and pro-longed. I flew from London to Belfast, rented a new, blue Ford Cortina, and drove to Londonderry where I had been assigned. As I entered the Bogside area, home to the most militant IRA people, a hooded man pointing a rifle ran in front of me, forcing me to stop. Before I could do anything, my car contained three other armed men, all wearing face masks, as I had not locked the doors. Rapidly, I told them who I was, more significantly that I was actually on my way to see the IRA chief in Derry. (The rebels against British occupation refuse to call the city "Londonderry," preferring to use its historic name, "Derry.") The armed men assured me that all they wanted was my car and my driving license, and the car would be returned that evening. Accustomed to being seen in battered jalopies, the men apparently figured that my bright rented car, with registration numbers traceable to Hertz, was less conspicuous to the security forces. I was taken to a house in the Bogside, put under a single armed guard—just a teenager, but I think he would have shot had I attempted to escape. During the long wait, I saw a platoon of familiar Grenadier Guards patrol down the street, and I could have bolted; nevertheless I considered it wiser to sit tight in case shooting broke out. The house in which I was kept was of prefabricated design, meaning any bullets would pierce the thin walls. At about 7 p.m., there was a single gunshot. My guard shouted, "Hit the deck!" and we flattened ourselves. After a few minutes of silence I peeped over the front window ledge— and there was my car. No people in sight. The gunshot was a way of getting everybody down on the ground so there were no witnesses as to who was getting out of my car. My guard left, and so did I.

I inspected the car inside and out, and underneath as best I could, just in case it had a bomb hidden. My sheepskin coat had been taken from the luggage compartment; otherwise, the car was perfectly clean. From the odometer, I calculated that around four hundred miles had been driven by the IRA men, probably taking a wounded man to Dublin or getting a consignment of arms and ammunition. Uptight and hungry, and for the time wanting nothing more to do with Northern Ireland, I drove over the border into the Republic of Ireland, booked into a posh hotel, had a large brandy and dinner, and went to bed. It was too late to check in with my newsroom or call home. The next morning I called London and received the calm response from the news editor: "We wondered what had happened to you." I called home but did not tell Jean what had happened so as not to concern her. But my paper insisted that I write a story about my kidnapping. That Sunday, when Jean and I were reading the newspapers under the cherry tree in the garden of our converted farmhouse home, Pinchloafe House, in Langley Burrell, Wiltshire, I noticed her come across the article on an inside page.

"So that's what happens to you when you're in Northern Ireland," she said casually. There the matter ended, except that a month later, I received a small package from the Royal Mail containing my driving license along with a note explaining that it had been found in a postal box in Liverpool.

As I've remarked, I never wanted to be a foreign correspondent, preferring to take care of family, but I was sent overseas in 1972—and bumped into the Shah of Iran. My assignment from the *Sunday Times* was to go to the Iran-Iraq border and report on the huge exodus of Shiite people being pushed out by Saddam Hussein (a Sunni), who claimed that they were Iranians originally and wanted them gone. I wondered why I was being sent and not the more knowledgeable correspondents on staff. When

X marks the apartment in Bath, Somerset, UK, where Derek was born in 1930.

Derek's wartime school in Priddy, Somerset, with the old Norman Church in the background

School picture of Derek on the day of the King of England's Coronation in 1937.

On leave, Father in RAF uniform with sons Garth (right) and Derek, 1941.

My mother (Bettine Eden) in the garden of her home in Freemantle, Austrialia, just before her stroke.

Jean Crane at 21 just before her marriage to Derek.

Jean on a garden trolley with her three sons (from left) Edgar, Clive, and Stephen, Manchester, 1961.

Jean Humphry at her desk, 1953.

Derek and Ann at Niagara Falls
during happy times, 1983.

Gretchen and Derek relaxing
beside the conference pool,
Kyoto, Japan, 1992.

Gretchen and Derek celebrating
at the 2000 World Conference in
Boston where Derek received the
Saba Medal for service to the cause.

Selling right to die books at the 1985
American Book Fair in Dallas.

Derek at 14.

Derek addressing Arizonans for
Death With Dignity, 1989.

Cartoon of Derek Humphry by David
Levine, *New York Review of Books*
(March 5, 1992).

Display of the books that made Hemlock famous, 1993.

I arrived at Khosravy, the scene was almost biblical—thousands of people on coaches, many others with donkeys and mule carts winding their way through the mountains to safety with fellow Shiites in Iran. The Iranian government had well-organized tent facilities and food awaiting the refugees, which they were keen for me to write about. On the second day, I spotted the Shah walking in a field nearby, went over to him, and introduced myself. Immediately he launched into a bitter attack on the policies of the *Times* and the *Sunday Times* for never giving him credit for how he was improving Iran, how good an ally he was to America and Britain, and that he was getting no outside help in this sudden, mass exodus of some sixty thousand people. The tirade went on for about twenty minutes, and I knew then why I, the homeboy, had been allotted this assignment. Foreign correspondents are extremely fussy about what nation stamps are on their passports and who they are known to have talked to. I was the innocent abroad; anyway, political ramifications did not bother me. The Shah and I kept walking as he expelled his wrath. "The West always helps pro-Socialist, dictatorial societies and not us," he ranted. "If it was a police state, everybody would help." When this diatribe expired, he became a normal person, and I was able to start an ordinary interview regarding the human tragedy going on around us. In spite of the Shah's other failings, which we learned about over the next decade, he was doing his utmost in this particular situation with temporary shelter and food for the refugees. "But I want a permanent solution for each family," he told me.

Chapter 8

TERMINAL ILLNESS

I N THE MIDDLE OF all the professional activity and family happiness, disaster struck. Jean found a lump in her breast. In the 1970s, there was little awareness of the need for women to have mammograms for early detection of cancer. When the lump was found, it must have been fairly well advanced. Four of Jean's aunts had died of breast cancer, thus she knew and often spoke about the possibility of her getting it as well. But not, she reckoned, until her sixties as was the case with her aunts, and perhaps by then there would be a cure. She was forty-one. Within days, she was in the hospital for examination, and it was found that the cancer was already well advanced. She was kept on the operating table, and a radical mastectomy was performed.

As she emerged from the anesthesia, I was at her side. Hazily, she asked me if the breast had been removed. Reluctantly, I had no choice but to say that it had. Her face seemed to collapse with shock and she burst into tears. Quickly, the nurses gave her more sedatives, hastening her back to sleep. I staggered out of the recovery ward to fall into Edgar's arms, crying like a child.

The medical profession went into high action to try to save her life. Radiation and chemotherapies seemed to help for a few months, but then pains began to develop in her bones, showing it had now become bone cancer. Jean fought every way, medically and psychologically, to beat the disease. She dressed brightly, careful to cover up the surgical scars and radiation burns, and dealt with people in her pleasant manner as though nothing had happened. She wanted only closest family and friends to know.

Edgar and Clive did everything possible to help and cheer their mother, doing household chores and visiting her during the spells when she was in the hospital. Unfortunately, Stephen was going through his period of teenage growing problems, adoption confusion, and racial identity. His rebellious attitude grew worse after leaving school, gaining and losing several jobs. Jean's terminal illness of course added hugely to the strain on the family. Edgar and Clive had become resentful of Stephen's upsetting behavior. In one temper tantrum, Stephen kicked in all the panels of a fairly new little car we owned. Then came an emotional flashpoint, when I knew I had to act.

Jean refused something he had asked for, at which point he screamed at her, "Why don't you hurry up and die!" Jean and the other boys were appalled.

I told Stephen, by now sixteen: "Get packed. You're leaving home." Immediately I drove with him into London and across town to the Notting Hill ghetto. There we went to the home of Mrs. J. R. Pugh, a huge, lovable "market mamma" type who took boarders and foster children of all races into her homely house in Old Oak Road. Although I have forgotten how, I had met this wonderful West Indian woman during earlier racial upsets in Notting Hill. Always simmering on her giant stove was a big black pot of nutritious soup, from which her "family" had to feed themselves. I asked Mrs. Pugh to take in Stephen as a boarder if I paid her the lodging fee of five pounds and fifty pence a week. She was warm and welcoming to Stephen. He seemed happy with the sudden change. At least now he was out of the well-to-do white ghetto and could experience how poorer people, also with racial identity problems, coped with them. As he worked as an office boy in central London, it was easier for him to get to work. Later, he went to live at Dashiki, also in Notting Hill, which was a hostel for homeless youths run by an acquaintance of mine, Vince Hines. He was always needing money, clothing, and fees for his art college, which I continued supplying until he was eighteen. It couldn't go on, so at that point I told Stephen: "That's it. You are now on your own. I will never give you another penny. You're welcome home any time, but don't ask for money anymore." And to his credit, he never has. Jean forgave him for his terrible outburst, and he came home for some weekends before she died.

After a year of fighting the disease, Jean asked me very firmly to find out just what her prospects were. She felt the doctors were deceiving her, for the best of motives. Jean was the sort of person who needed to know the truth, no matter how harsh. At this point, she had to spend most of her time in bed because of back pains. One day in the hospital, I persuaded two of her doctors to see me alone in their office. I told them that Jean wanted the truth, and so did I. We were the sort of people who could not live in ignorance of the realities.

"You must be ready for the worst," said one doctor. "She's going to die. We will do everything we can for her, but it does not look good."

We took Jean home by ambulance and tucked her into bed, now placed in the living room so that she felt a part of family life. After we had settled down, Jean asked me, "What did the doctors say?" I had to put a hold on my emotions. How do you tell a person, your beloved wife, that death for her is close? But we had always been honest with each other, thus I knew she would not accept any half-truths.

"They say there is nothing more they can do. You will die as the bone cancer spreads." There followed the most awful silence I have ever experienced. For three days Jean said nothing. In a desultory way she picked at meals brought to her. I was devastated at what I had done, apparently making a horrible mistake in asking the doctors—as Jean had requested—and passing on to her the fatal news. On the third day of silence, slight relief for my anguish came in the form of a phone call from a friend asking how Jean was. I told her of the awful silence.

"She's in mourning for herself," she said.

Strangely, that explanation somewhat relieved the pain of my presumed blunder. I had never heard this expression before. You can imagine my relief when on the fourth day Jean woke up and said, "Good morning," and life resumed as before! Later that morning she told me that now that she had accepted she was going to die, she was going to make the best of what time was left. And she did, as is related in the little book I later wrote about it, *Jean's Way* (Quartet Books, 1978).

Stephen has made his own way in the ruthless world in London, with a steady job and a bachelor apartment. We remain firm friends. I helped him get in touch with his biological mother in 1974, which led to the discovery and friendship with two brothers and a sister. Perhaps because of how he was treated as a baby and toddler, he finds it difficult to make long-term relationships with women. Young black women are attracted to him because many love lighter-colored skins than their own, plus he is good-looking, well groomed, polite, and well mannered. Two lengthy relationships with black women have produced a son and a daughter from each but not marriage. He dotes on both children. If Jean had lived to see the fine man Stephen became, despite the upsets, she would be pleased and proud.

Chapter 9

JEAN'S WAY OF DYING

J EAN FACED HER ONCOMING death with considerable courage, determined to make the best of what little life she had left. In mid-1974 her illness took a turn for the worse, and doctors told me that she might not last more than a few days. But using her powerful will to live, plus superb medical care, pain management, and nursing at the Churchill Hospital in Oxford, Jean pulled out of the crisis. Yet she was a changed person. What began the alteration was the experience of her mother's death, as well as watching other people die during her long months spent in cancer wards. Five years earlier, her mother had died of lung cancer in Jean's presence, and it was a "bad death" for two reasons. First, Beatrice Crane either did not fully realize she was dying or refused to contemplate it. Secondly, she was in unremitting and untreated pain at home during the final stages. Her mother's physical pain and psychic anguish as she died had so deeply affected Jean that she privately resolved that such an unprepared death would never happen to her. During her own illness Jean had talked of the sadness of witnessing the deaths of other patients in the hospital, with the distressed families almost always arriving in the middle of the night, too late. When I returned to the Churchill Hospital one day, I found Jean sitting up in bed, temporarily recovered from the near-death experience. My epiphany was at hand.

"Derek," she said, taking a deep breath. "I simply don't want to go on living like this. It's been pretty bad this week, and I want you to do something for me so that if I decide I want to die, I can do it on my own terms and exactly when I choose.

"The one thing that worries me is that I won't be in any position to make the right decision, what with my being knocked senseless by all these drugs. I might be too daft to know whether I'm doing the right thing or not, but I shall have a good idea when I've had enough of the pain. So I want you to promise me that when I ask you if this is the right time to kill myself, you will give me an honest answer one way or another, and we must understand, both you and I, that I'll do it right at that very moment. You won't question my right, and you will give me the means to do it."

After a pause to recover from this surprise request, I told her that if our positions were reversed and I was the one dying of cancer, I would be asking her to help me die. It was an instinctive reply from the heart because I had never previously considered the matter. As with many other couples in their early forties who are busy raising teenagers, thoughts of death and how dying might be handled had not been considered. At the time I had no idea that this brief conversation would completely alter the course of my life. So unprepared was I for what Jean termed her "escape hatch" that I had to ask Jean what she actually wanted me to do, other than agree to her assisted suicide. We were not aware of any such thing as a euthanasia movement—it was not then a subject of public discussion—thus we had no preconceived views on the subject.

Jean, on the other hand, had thought the matter through carefully. "Find a doctor who will give us the lethal drugs with which I can take my life," she said in her usual, straightforward manner. "When I'm ready to go, you will hand them over without argument." I agreed.

Almost immediately, I sought out a physician in London who had been helpful to me some years previously when I was doing investigative reporting on administrative problems in the British Health Service. I had a hunch that this was the man with the intelligence and the compassion to help Jean and me.

"Dr. Joe"—the only clue I have ever revealed as to his identity—heard my plea for lethal drugs with which Jean could kill herself. He questioned me closely about her medical condition and concluded: "She has no quality of life left." Almost casually, Dr. Joe telephoned the chief pharmacist at the hospital where he had privileges and asked which drugs would be most lethal for this purpose. The conversation over, reluctant to write out a prescription which could give him away to the authorities, he went to his drug cabinet and gave me a mixture of two substances, with instructions how to use them. They were secobarbital and codeine. "Never reveal that I did this," instructed Dr. Joe. We shook hands on this pact of silence.

Both of us were about to be guilty of the crime of assisted suicide under Section Two of the Suicide Act of 1961, and liable upon conviction for up to fourteen years imprisonment. Joe was also guilty of prescribing drugs to a person who was not his patient. How strange that the same act that had ruled that Jean's suicide was no longer a felony caused people like me trouble. Suicide and attempted suicide were decriminalized in 1961 in the UK, but assisted suicide was left standing. Thus we were perpetrating a crime in order to carry out something that was not a crime. This struck me as ludicrous. Immediately after Jean's request, I studied this particular law and noticed a caveat in it that a prosecution could not be directly brought by the police—as with most crimes—but only with the permission of the director of public prosecutions (DPP). Having written about the administration of justice for the *Sunday Times* for many years, I knew that the then DPP, Alistair Hetherington, was a man of humane and liberal tendencies. So I decided that the necessity of helping Jean to die was worth the small risk of prosecution.

To make Jean's last years more pleasant, we moved out of London to a pretty village in the southern Cotswolds. The three-hundred-year-old stone house we purchased included the grocery store for the village of Langley Burrell, in Wiltshire. The former farmhouse had the cute name of "Pinchloafe House," which had something to do with it once also being the village bakery. It was the same area I had covered when a young news reporter for the *Bristol Evening World*. Jean took huge pleasure in running this little store even though she had no previous retail sales experience. For about a year, there was ample time for relaxation and reflection. Jean took a third chemotherapy, giving her a welcome remission. Nine months elapsed between the making of the assisted suicide pact and Jean's death, but in the meantime it was never discussed between us, although Jean would occasionally tell her girlfriends that she was "not planning to go to the end with this." Apparently these friends, who knew Jean's determined character, accepted these remarks and remembered them. These fairly offhand statements were fortuitous for me, as it turned out, because when the police went looking for evidence against me three years later, they showed the suicide was Jean's plan and not mine. In early 1975, Jean's cancer returned with a vengeance, spreading from her bones to other vital organs. Back in the hospital, her doctors told her that there were no more treatments available for her condition; she was going to die. They promised to manage her pain and offered her the choice between dying in the hospital or at home. With her self-deliverance plan in mind, she opted for an ambulance to take her home. There were no tears, just a calm acceptance that the end was near. It seemed to me that Jean had already mourned for herself. Accompanying her stash of painkillers was a large bottle of what the British call "Brompton cocktail" and Americans call "hospice mix," which is a concoction of narcotic analgesics made up by trial and error to quell the pain of the particular patient. In overdose it is lethal (therefore, it could have been used in suicide instead of Dr. Joe's pills).

During the next three days, I noticed that Jean was saying good-bye to people and tidying up those parts of the bedroom that she could reach. This was the time to consider whether I was still willing to go through with my part of the pact; I resolved that if she asked me, I would. I was caught in an awful dichotomy of, on the one hand, not wanting her to die and yet on the other, willing to respond to her desire to kill herself to avoid further suffering. The danger now was that Jean's bones might break with the slightest strain, which did happen in the week before her end when she let a washbowl slip. She bent forward instinctively to catch it before the water soaked the bedclothes, and snapped several ribs. Now she was bed-bound, unable to reach the bathroom, and this handicap seemed to be her benchmark for the conclusion of her life. Jean insisted on knowing every detail of her illness, how far the cancer had spread into vital organs, and the huge amount of painkilling drugs she was consuming to exist. Not being able any longer to go to the bathroom put the cap on her deteriorating quality of life. She knew the end was near.

All those around her were amazed at her grace and calm as she was approaching death. I alone knew of her suicide plan at this point, although a few days before her death, Jean confided to our sons what her intentions were. Generally stunned by the impending loss of their dear mother, nevertheless they understood because they had helped to care for her, witnessed her moments of agony, and sympathized with her suffering. The teenagers remained quiet and supportive.

When she awoke on March 29, Jean's pain was so intense she was unable to move. Quickly, I brought her painkillers, and once they had taken effect she was then able cautiously to sit up in bed, propped up by numerous pillows.

"Is this the day?" Jean quietly asked me.

For a few moments, I was paralyzed by the awesome nature of the question. She had decided to die now. Although not unexpected, it was nevertheless traumatic to have to give permission to the person whom you love most in the world to kill herself. Part of our original pact had been that Jean would not act without my agreement in case her massive doses of painkillers clouded her judgment. Now I had to decide whether I concurred. I prevaricated for a few moments by discussing Jean's present worsening condition, which might necessitate a quick return to the hospital, and then conceded that perhaps the time had come.

"The doctors say there is nothing else to be done," I said.

Sensing my acceptance, Jean immediately stated: "I shall die at one o'clock. You must give me the overdose and then go into the garden and not return for an hour. We'll say our last good-bye here but I don't want you actually to see me die."

We spent the morning talking about our life together. Jean insisted on going over plans for my future, including her permission for me to marry again as soon as I wished. Jean also made me promise to travel north to tell her father just how she had died.

"I don't want him to think I died in pain or like a vegetable," she said. "He suffered enough when Mother died because no one would make any decisions. I want him to be sure to know that I died this way."

During that last morning, Jean raised the troublesome matter of my breaking the law by helping her end her life.

"Don't worry," I assured her. "I can handle it. There is not the slightest doubt in my mind that if this is the way you wish to die, then it is my duty to help you."

As one o'clock approached, a calm and collected Jean asked me to get her the drugs, which I had decided were best taken in a large mug of white coffee, plentifully laced with sugar to reduce the bitter taste. Two of our sons, Edgar and Clive, were present in the house; the third, Stephen, was away in London, working. The previous evening Jean had sent me to the market on a trumped-up errand, then calling into her bedroom the two teenagers. She told them what she was planning the next day and they said their good-byes. Now, as I passed them in the living room carrying the lethal coffee, I told them: "I think she's close to death." Slumped in armchairs, buried in their own grief and confusion, they said nothing.

Jean asked if this cup of coffee was it. I nodded. "If you drink this you will die." She was incredibly calm and collected. I was the one alternately crying and on the verge of panic.

After we embraced on the bed for the last time, had a final hug and a kiss, I sat down on the bedside chair. Jean immediately took the mug and gulped its contents swiftly. As I took the empty mug from her, she just had time to say: "Good-bye, my love" before she passed out. I ignored her request to leave the room, considering it better to remain and ensure that nothing went wrong.

Within seconds, the drugs had knocked Jean out and she lay breathing heavily, occasionally snoring. At one point, Jean vomited—we did not know then of the importance of anti-emetics to prevent sickness caused by swallowing so much toxic medication—and I was terrified that she had not kept down enough of the deadly potion. I prepared myself to stifle her with a pillow if she showed signs of awakening because I had resolved that she would not awaken from such a well-prepared dying. Fortunately for both of us, within fifty minutes the drugs worked, and respiration ceased. Jean lay peacefully at rest after all her suffering. I sat at her bedside, dazed with the loss yet also filled with admiration for the courageous, determined, and dignified manner of her death. The swift finality of it stunned me—one moment she was here, next she was gone.

All this was later to have unforeseen repercussions.

Chapter 10

OFF TO CALIFORNIA

T HE *Sunday Times* was always scouting for fresh writing talent, either from home or abroad. Among others, the paper gave a trial to Venkat Narajan, a promising young Indian journalist who was attached to the *Times of India*. He was so raw in communications and styles that I was "assigned" to him to help him become familiar. Once he had a grasp on the English way of doing things, he became a most useful journalist. Venkat had a clubfoot that, he told me, was the only reason he was in journalism. His brothers and sisters had no such handicap and were thus able to work in the family's fields. Because he could not follow the plow, he was the only person in his family given a college education. Another young journalist was Walter Isaacson, who had brief spells at the *Sunday Times* after Harvard and Oxford. Undecided about his future, Walter returned to his hometown of New Orleans and worked for the local newspaper. I spent the 1978 Mardi Gras celebrations with him, made more enjoyable as he explained the traditions and ceremonies, and crashed in his apartment in the Latin Quarter. Walter asked me whether I thought he should join the *Sunday Times* or *Time* magazine, both of which were eager to have him. I recommended my newspaper, naturally. Fortunately, he did not take my advice, went to *Time*, and gradually rose through the ranks to become managing editor. Amazingly industrious, Walter also found time to write best-selling biographies of Henry Kissinger, Benjamin Franklin, and Albert Einstein.

We did not know in early 1978 that the *Sunday Times* in the next decade would go through drastic changes in editorship (Evans gone), ownership—from Thomson to Murdoch—a yearlong strike, and production difficulties. It was not a happy, secure place to work. I realized that the golden era of this great newspaper was ending, as all golden eras do. I was "the first rat off the sinking ship" in 1978 when I transferred to the *Los Angeles Times*. Very few writers of that era remained at the London paper. It had been my best twelve of thirty-five years in staff journalism—and I needed change.

After the disciplined, fast-moving style of British journalism, I found it difficult to adapt to the laid-back, slower way by which the *Los Angeles Times* was run. The newsroom then was hugely overstaffed, and it was difficult to discover who was in command. (A former chief editor of the paper once described running the paper as similar to "trying to steer an aircraft carrier by putting my hands in the water.") Just before I arrived, the managing editor, Mr. Thomas, had spent a holiday in England and had the idea that I should mainly write articles comparing how the two countries organized policing, prison, and civil liberties. I tried, but the results were not impressive because in the neighborhoods, grassroots, and courts, there are extremely different social forces at work. Copyeditors to whom I submitted these articles pointed out this disparity, and I had to agree with them.

But I did get eight articles published in my year at the paper, which from what I could observe, was a normal workload for a journalist here. I wrote about the uncomfortable relationships between the Los Angeles police and the people in Watts, which so often resulted in violent encounters. Short of ideas at one stage, I asked editor Thomas what he thought I might tackle next. "I don't know, Derek," he responded. "You're a good journalist; you find something." It was this attitude of intellectual indifference after the sharpness, the constant intellectual debate about what was news, of the London paper that I found dispiriting. (Today the newsroom of the *Los Angeles Times* is a great deal smaller and better run, and the resulting newspaper is of much higher quality. I seem to have hit a bad patch.)

The next article I chose was to pick out of the bulging Los Angeles police files a run-of-the-mill murder—which had no scandal attached and had received no publicity—and trace the lives of both victim and the perpetrator. Upon investigation, the case turned out to have some odd features. The killer was a house painter with no criminal record, but he needed more money than he could earn. First, he dosed himself with alcohol laced with aspirin and then went to rob a jewelry shop. The seventy-six-year-old woman minding the store noticed him stealing watches and shouted for help. The robber grabbed her, pulled an ice pick from his pocket, and stabbed her to death. He walked out with only a couple of cheap watches, ignoring the hundreds of dollars in the cash register. By a fluke, nobody was in the shopping plaza, thus he walked away unseen. Not being a regular criminal, his fingerprints did not appear in any police file, so he remained undetected. The killer went on with his life for the next three years, but his conscience troubled him; his internal torment grew so great that he could rarely sleep. When he decided to turn himself in, he drove to the police station nearest to the scene of the crime and went in late on a Friday afternoon. "I want to confess to a murder," he told the desk sergeant.

"Could you come back Monday morning?" the astonished killer was told. "We have no detectives on duty now." He did come back, was listened to this time, and ended up being sentenced to five years to life for second-degree murder. I also traced what had happened to the family of the dead woman, how the store and the whole plaza was nearly put out of business when the horrible crime became known. The *Times* would give almost unlimited space to a finely detailed article of this nature.

My last investigation for the *LA Times* was into the nature and reality of dying in America. My ulterior motive for this was that *Jean's Way* was due to be published in New York in the fall of 1979, thus I wanted to be well acquainted with the American situation on death and dying as well as meet the main people involved. I spent a day with Elizabeth Kubler-Ross at her Frank Lloyd Wright–designed home in Flossmoor, outside Chicago. That morning, I was deeply impressed with her convictions, dedication, and lovely humanity on such a serious subject as dying. Then she made a light lunch in a kitchen where, if you weren't careful, you could fall into the indoor swimming pool. Resuming our discussion in the afternoon, she launched into a lengthy lecture on how she could tell exactly when a person would die by examining drawings done in childhood. Dr. Kubler-Ross also believed in life after death—but not because of religious belief, so it seemed. I left her house extremely disillusioned with the person who was the most well-known and respected person on death and dying in America. Probably this was due to the fact that I am—as somebody once remarked to me—one of the least metaphysical persons in the world.

Dr. Kubler-Ross had written in one of her books, *Questions and Answers on Death and Dying* (Scribner, 1974), that she did not dispute the right of dying people—provided they had put their affairs in order—to take their own lives. When later I started the Hemlock Society, I did not expect her to be against its philosophy. Nevertheless, she told a newspaper in Los Angeles that she was against groups that spread the gospel of euthanasia and the right to commit suicide.

"To kill or abbreviate the life of a cancer patient is a problem not the patient has, but one the caretaker has," she was quoted as saying. "They cannot tolerate to watch the suffering or deal with whatever unfinished business in their own lives. They try to terminate a life under the disguise of mercy and that is not mercy. Today dying does not have to be a nightmare. Dying does not have to be painful" (*Los Angeles Daily News*, October 28, 1983).

To me, Dr. Kubler-Ross was missing three vital points: first, how does a dying person—weak and bed-bound probably—end their life without help? Second, pain can mostly be controlled nowadays, but what about decisions to die based on an awful quality of life? And finally, the fact that Hemlock wanted to change the law so that family and friends did not have to assist the suicide. It would be physician-assisted suicide under tight rules, as now in Oregon. In my experience, her claim that caretakers of dying persons helped them to die to relieve themselves of the burden was never proven.

For two months I toured the US, talking to doctors, nurses, medical scientists, ethicists, philosophers, even funeral home directors. One expert seemed to lead to another. Oncologists provided the most realistic examples of dying as their cancer-ridden patients faced troubling ends. Many hinted that they would not go through such difficulties if they contracted cancer;

suicide would be their choice. The result was a series of three articles in the *Los Angeles Times* with the umbrella heading of "The Quality of Dying in America." California was the center of a great deal of my interviewing because it had in 1976 passed the first "living will" law in the world. Although I did not realize it at the time, knowing these people and where they stood on the euthanasia issue enabled me shortly to get the Hemlock Society off to a flying start.

Chapter 11

A BOOK'S INSPIRATION

Although family and friends all knew of the way Jean had died, nobody reported my crime to the police. Most did not know it was a felony to assist a suicide. The treating doctor was called and signed a death certificate giving "carcinomatosis" as the cause of death, not realizing that she had accelerated her end. Jean was quietly cremated and, as was her wish, there was no funeral or memorial service. Subsequently, I was asked many times if I ever regretted helping Jean kill herself. "No," I would answer. "I would feel guilty if I had refused her request and allowed her to continue suffering." Although only a small circle of close family and friends knew of my action, none treated me differently.

After a period of mourning, I took Jean's deathbed advice to get on with my life as soon as possible. I went back to work at the *Sunday Times* and gradually got involved in a social whirl in London. During Jean's illness, I had not considered writing about it, although some of my writer colleagues suggested doing so. But as I gradually managed to distance myself from the sadness of her death, I thought about writing a long magazine article about

the experience of helping a loved one to die. After my marriage
to Ann Wickett a year later, she urged me to write a book, not
an article, about Jean's life and death, and—as she was unemployed—offered to help. An American who had studied psychology at Boston and Toronto Universities, now a mature student
at England's Shakespeare Institute, Ann was able to provide certain womanly insights to the text that I could not. So, in my spare
time, we sat down to put together a book that was to be Stage
Two of the drastic alteration of my life. I dictated the book;
Ann probed into the background and motives of the story as I
described it and suggested additions. It was a fruitful partnership
but a testing one emotionally for both Ann and me. During the
investigation and writing, Ann had inevitably become intimately
aware of her new husband's previous partner of twenty-two
years, and comparisons were inevitable. Reliving the agony of
watching Jean suffer and then kill herself was traumatic for me,
making tears commonplace as the typewriter clicked and the
story unfolded in a stark, no-holds-barred fashion.

But when the book was ready in 1977, finding a publisher—
or even a literary agent—proved difficult. My agent, Elaine
Greene, then one of the top agents in London, refused to market
the book, saying that I should regard it as a cathartic exercise and
move on to my next one. I showed the manuscript to a few author
friends, and they suggested that I trash it. So I started looking
for a publisher myself. Several London firms were quick to read
it because I was an established, prize-winning author with what
the English call a "good address" at the *Sunday Times*. But they
were equally quick to return the manuscript. "Too harrowing"
or "not saleable" was their cumulative opinion. The book was
also shown to several American publishers, who also rejected it.
"Bring us your next book," they all said approvingly.

I knew in my heart that this was an important story with a message and that it was marketable. Having been on holiday in America and studied the bookstores there, I knew that a book on death and dying did have a market. *Death Be Not Proud* (Harper & Row, 1949) by John Gunther was a classic example, and the books of Elizabeth Kubler-Ross underlined this. In desperation, I took the manuscript to London's newest and smallest publisher, Quartet Books, where I knew that one editor, William Miller, was more perceptive, liberal, and freethinking than most of his profession. Miller had published my trailblazing book *Police Power and Black People* in 1972. This paperback original, by the way, got an enormous amount of publicity in print, TV, and radio but sold pathetically, and many thousands were pulped, which taught me that a lot of media noise does not necessarily amount to big bookstore sales.

Within twenty-four hours Miller called back and said: "Of course I'll publish it, but you must stand by the legal consequences and be prepared to defend your actions in the media and the courts if necessary." Accustomed to hostile publicity from my previous books on race, police, and civil liberties, I said I would do whatever was necessary when the book came out. Even given Miller's enthusiasm, the publisher paid a mere five hundred pounds royalty advance and did not bother to keep the customary publishers' share of the film, paperback, and foreign rights. They were to regret their miscalculation.

Unknown to me at the time, three events had been reshaping the right to die movement. First, the Karen Ann Quinlan case in 1976 in New Jersey alerted the nonmedical world to the fact that people who usually died were now being kept alive by super technology. The court case reverberated around the world as people were astonished—and horror-struck—that medicine was now in a new era. This young woman, virtually brain-dead, was being kept barely alive by artificial tube feeding and air supply. The reaction in California, for instance, was to pass the world's first "living will" law the same year, through which people could choose to sign an advance directive saying they would not want to live in such a way should they be in the same situation. Within a few years, all the states in the US had legalized some form of advance directive for end-of-life medical care.

A British playwright had anticipated this phenomenon by writing *Whose Life Is It Anyway?* Brian Clark got it shown on BBC Television in 1972 and then spent another six years trying to place it on a theatrical stage. When he succeeded in getting the Mermaid Theatre in London to stage the play in March 1978, it became a blockbuster. Luckily for me, *Jean's Way* was published the same month, and I was invited to opening night. Fiction based on fact, Clark's play was very much about the medical-ethical dilemma of the moment, whereas my book was a nonfiction memoir peeking into the future of the same subject. Almost the same age, Clark and I got on well and appeared together on several television and radio shows, discussing the implications of our work. *Whose Life Is It Anyway?* had a good run in London and went on to be a smash on Broadway, where the lead part was played alternately by a male or female actor. In 1983, it was released as a Hollywood movie with Richard Dreyfuss playing the part of the sculptor who became a tetraplegic in a car crash, now asking the doctors to let him die as his quality of life was below what he desired.

When the Hemlock Society hosted the World Right to Die Conference in San Francisco in 1988, I invited Brian Clark to speak on the effect of his play. He described how it had been translated into twenty-two languages, but never into Russian. Soviet Russia was fiercely anti-euthanasia—even today in modern Russia it is a delicate subject, with no progress in sight.

When *Jean's Way* hit the bookstores in March of 1978, it was an immediate sellout, gone in five days. It earned a wave of publicity, nationally and internationally, considerably helped by a powerful television documentary shown on the Credo series by London Weekend Television. The book reviewers were positive about it. It had overturned a dark stone in a gray area of English institutional and publishing thinking—revealing that a section of the public is not afraid to read about actual dying and death. The book went on to be published in paperback in Britain and Australia, in hardback in America, and have editions in paperback from major publishers such as Harper & Row and Dell. There have been five translations into major languages. Thirty years later, I offer *Jean's Way* in a digital edition, and it sells modestly. In 2008, it was published in translations in Turkey and Mexico. Immediately as it hit the bookstores, I found myself defending assisted suicide in public, arguing on television with notable opponents such as Dame Cecily Saunders, the pioneer of the modern hospice movement, and Malcolm Muggeridge, the raconteur and popular philosopher. Ludovic Kennedy devoted the whole of his immensely popular talk show *Tonight* to me, about Jean in particular and the philosophy behind the right to die in general. Intense and widespread criticism—notably from church and hospice leaders—of my action in helping Jean to die was offset by enormous support. People from all over the world wrote saying either that they, too, had helped a loved one die or that they would want to be able to get that help if ever needed. People sometimes stopped me in the street to shake my hand. Hospice leaders said that if Jean had been in their care, she would not have wanted to commit suicide because they would have managed her pain. Not so. Jean had adequate pain control from a bunch of caring physicians. She took her life probably about a month before it would have ended naturally because she was concerned not with the pain management but about the quality of her life in those remaining days. "Quality of life" is something few doctors will talk about before or after a patient's death. It is not really their business, being essentially the patient's choice.

When the media had no more "angles" for stories, within a few days, they asked the director of public prosecutions what he was going to do about this clear confession to a crime in *Jean's Way*. Prompted by the *Daily Mirror*, he ordered a police inquiry so that he could—as the Suicide Act, 1961, specified—make a decision on whether or not to prosecute. Within days, Wiltshire police detectives traveled to London to meet me by arrangement in my lawyer's office. There I handed them a written confession to the crime, with the addendum that I would plead guilty if taken to court and ask for its mercy. The detectives officially warned me that I was under investigation for the crime of assisted suicide and read me the British equivalent of my Miranda Rights.

The police accepted my confession but followed up with a barrage of questions about the doctor who had supplied the lethal drugs. They seemed keener to "get" this person than get me! Repeatedly, I told them I would never reveal the name of the doctor, so they were wasting their time. After an hour, the detectives, who did not seem to be antagonistic but merely doing their duty, gave up and left. In every other respect I cooperated with the police, giving permission to interview any members of the family, friends, and Jean's treating physicians, who, of course, were unaware of the suicide. What the police found was that this accelerated death was entirely Jean's plan, with me as an accessory. Six months later, the public prosecutor ruled that he was exercising his discretion allowed by law and would not prosecute. Of course, he had only my word that a crime had been committed—a person may not be convicted of a felony on their admission alone. There has to be corroborating evidence. By this time I was living in California, working for the *Los Angeles Times*, but I had left word with my lawyer and the prosecutor that if the decision was to take me to court, I would return voluntarily to Britain, avoiding messy extradition proceedings.

I never met the novelist and thinker Arthur Koestler, who is best known for his anti-Communist novel *Darkness at Noon* (Macmillan, 1940), but I have reason to be grateful to him. He selected *Jean's Way* to be the best book of 1978 and commented in the *Observer*, a quality London Sunday newspaper, that it was ". . . a powerful plea for voluntary euthanasia—the individual's right to death in peace and dignity." Koestler's endorsement at last convinced the doubters—among them some of my journalist colleagues—that my book had merit. What I did not know at the time—because he had never written about it in his numerous books—was that Koestler firmly believed in euthanasia. In 1983 Koestler, aged seventy-seven, suffering from Parkinson's disease and leukemia, took his own life with an overdose of Tuinal. It was no surprise because he was a vice president of the Voluntary Euthanasia Society in England and left a suicide note that ended by saying: "After a more or less steady decline . . . the process has now reached an acute state with added complications which make it advisable to seek self-deliverance now. . . . It is to Cynthia that I owe the relative peace and happiness in the last period of my life—and never before."

What was a surprise was that his wife, Cynthia, was found dead in a chair beside him in their home in London, having taken the same drug. Aged fifty-five, Cynthia was in perfect health. It was a planned death by her, for two days earlier she had taken their dog, David, to a vet to be put to sleep. Her suicide note included the statement: "I cannot live without Arthur, despite certain inner resources."

Enter Hemlock

Events began to unfold that turned me from being just a writer to also being an activist campaigner. All my life I had been interested in causes and had worked in campaigns in Britain to make police accountable for misdeeds, for racial equality, and for civil liberties. In Britain I was known as "a campaigning journalist," and in the US as an "advocacy journalist."

The Australian public has always shown a strong interest in euthanasia, so when fifty thousand copies of *Jean's Way* were printed in paperback there, it sold hugely, and I was invited to that country for a joint book promotion and lecture tour. What impressed me most were the audiences, young and old, of varying educational standards, who packed the meeting halls. "I must be saying something people want to hear," I mused. On my return to the US I had more invitations to speak to university groups, senior citizen clubs, and Unitarian churches.

When *Jean's Way* was published in the US in 1979, I was invited on all the major talk shows, television and radio, although the book only sold modestly. That year the Santa Monica bookstore Vroman's invited me to have a book signing, leaving me with the impression that the event was for *Jean's Way*. When I arrived at the store, I noticed a long line of people winding out of the store and around the block. Wow! I took my place at my signing table, piled with copies of my book, but things were strangely quiet. I noticed that every person in the line was walking up to the African American woman at a table nearby who was signing books. Not one person bought my book or even spoke to me. Fresh off the boat, so to speak, I did not know who this author was. I made inquiries and found that she was Maya Angelou, the black poet who is one of the most respected literary figures of the twentieth century, promoting her masterpiece *I Know Why the Caged Bird Sings.* I was out of my league! So I slipped away from Vroman's. It was another twelve years before I could get a bookstore audience anything like Ms. Angelou's, with *Final Exit.*

Yet the visibility for what was now developing into a major social cause for me was enormous. Easily able to contact me at the *Los Angeles Times,* people poured in requests for help in dying and for advice, and urged me to do something about changing the law, which was and still is just as punitive on the euthanasia issue in the United States as in Britain. The most frequent questions put to me were: what are the most lethal drugs, and where do you get them? The Voluntary Euthanasia Society in London told me that it had some five hundred Americans as members, and I was welcome to their names and addresses if I could use them.

The idea was developing in my mind that there ought to be an organization, similar to those in Britain and Australia, fighting for Americans' right to a chosen death. First I approached the two right to die groups in New York: Concern for Dying and the Society for the Right to Die (which later merged as Choice in Dying, and then faded away). I asked them to branch out from advanced directives into also advocating legal, medical, voluntary euthanasia, and assisted suicide. They declined, claiming America was not ready for this. I felt they were wrong because the evidence indicated a huge public interest. At dinner one evening in Santa Monica, I talked with Ann about my plan for a specialized group. She suggested it be called "Hemlock," and I agreed, adding the word "Society" as a clarification of what it was. Thus was born the Hemlock Society, America's first group fighting exclusively for assisted suicide and voluntary euthanasia for the terminally and irreversibly ill. Hemlock also distributed "advance directives" (living wills) as also being an additional precaution against being trapped on life-support equipment against one's wishes.

I was obliged to go forward with my Hemlock plan due to a meeting with Mike Wallace of CBS's *60 Minutes* program to talk about *Jean's Way*. As his film crew and I happened to be in London simultaneously, it was arranged to meet there. It was Mike's sixtieth birthday, so as we waited for the studio to be set up he took me to a little celebration luncheon in a Bayswater bistro. At the time, there was a raging controversy over whether it was right for an English euthanasia society to publish a "how-to" booklet entitled "A Guide to Self Deliverance." On camera, Mike asked me what I would do if this booklet was dropped (as it was later). Because of what I had been mulling over previously, I instinctively replied that I would form my own organization and publish a similar book. This public declaration of course now committed me to rapid action, announcing the foundation of Hemlock before the CBS program aired. At the time of this interview in 1979, Wallace did not betray any sympathy for the rapidly emerging euthanasia cause, but in recent years, as he has aged, he has been openly supportive, particularly through Dr. Jack Kevorkian's campaign.

At the height of the *Jean's Way* rumpus in London in 1978, the *Evening Standard* had asked me for a feature page article that appeared under the then fairly unusual headline of "The Right to Die with Dignity." In my article, though a novice in this field, I presented a four-point charter for legislation:

1. The patient must know the essentials of his situation, the available therapies, the alternative prognosis, and possibilities. He must be fully aware that euthanasia is irreversible death.
2. The patient must have voluntarily requested euthanasia, preferably repeatedly confirming that the present

situation and all available alternatives are unbearable
to him.

3. He must be incurable, with no possibility of alleviating his suffering in a manner acceptable to him. Death must, in his informed and considered opinion, be the only acceptable solution.

4. Euthanasia must be applied by the attending doctor.

Making allowances for the then poorly defined meaning of words such as "euthanasia," this appears to have been the first published charter for assisted suicide in the English-speaking world. (The Dutch had been working on such propositions for the previous five years.) Working from these ideas, two years later I drew up a draft charter for the aims and objectives of Hemlock, circulating it to dozens of professionals who I knew were interested in the subject. In essence, it said that Hemlock would provide information so that persons dying now could end their own lives with dignity, and also that, long-term, Hemlock would fight for reform of the law. It would be a nonprofit California educational corporation with a board of directors and a small staff. In California, where Hemlock—although a national organization from the outset—was to be based, suicide was not a crime, but under Penal Code 301 any form of assistance was felonious, punishable by up to fifteen years imprisonment. But as much as I and others researched, we could not find a single instance of an assisted suicide conviction under a law that had been in place since 1897. Although some warned me against starting what seemed to them to be a crazy, California pro-suicide group, I relied on my gut instincts and public relations skills to get it across to the law enforcement authorities and public opinion that this was assistance for the terminally ill only, purely on a voluntary basis, and the long-term aim was democratic law reform to permit the procedure under regulated circumstances. Thirty-seven other states had specific laws punishing assistance in suicide, and the remainder punished it as murder or manslaughter. Law reform on this scale, with such a controversial issue, was obviously a mountainous task, but from the start I told supporters that it would take probably twenty years to achieve. (I was wrong—it needs at least another twenty years.)

The original draft charter—or mission statement—of Hemlock, which I drew up as a result of two years of debate and study, reads as follows:

Hemlock's Charter Principles

1. Hemlock's objective is to promote a climate of public opinion which is tolerant of the right of people who are terminally ill to end their own lives in a planned manner.
2. Hemlock does not condone suicide for any primary emotional, traumatic or financial reasons in the absence of terminal illness. It approves of the work of all those involved in suicide prevention.
3. Hemlock will not encourage terminally ill people to end their lives, believing that this action, and its timing, to be an extremely personal decision, where possible taken in concert with family and friends.
4. A book providing information about methods and strategies of planned death with dignity will be supplied to members upon request. (This book is in preparation and not immediately available.)
5. Hemlock speaks only to those people of like mind who approach it out of mutual sympathy with its

goals. Views contrary to its own which are held by
other religions and philosophies are respected.

Those who received the draft charter were invited to a meeting on July 16, 1980, at the Westwood (Los Angeles) home of
Richard Scott, a physician and lawyer, who had told me of his
interest. About twenty people turned up to discuss the issue of
whether the US needed an organization fighting for the right
of a dying person to end their life and—more importantly—to
get help to do it. I had come to know them all while researching
my series of articles on "The Quality of Dying in America," so
I had a good idea where their sympathies and skills lay. For two
hours there was a lively discussion on the need for a group such
as Hemlock. Finally, when I called for a vote on the necessity
of such a group, acceptance was unanimous. Then I asked for
those who would join such a group to step forward. Only one
person did! Astonished, I asked the attendees why they could
on the one hand approve of such an organization and on the
other hand fail to support it? Some muttered that their legal,
medical, nursing, or psychological practices could be affected.
Others said their children attended Roman Catholic schools and
might meet resentment; a few worried that their homes might
get bombed by the same fanatics who were bombing abortion
clinics.

Only Dr. Gerald A Larue, at that time professor of religious
studies at the University of Southern California, offered to put
his name down for the new organization. "If we believe in a cause,
then we must be prepared to back it," he declared in the rich,
ringing voice that is his characteristic. Larue was well known
in California academic circles for his iconoclastic views of many
subjects, religious and otherwise. Many years earlier he had pioneered academic courses in "Death and Dying" that included all

aspects of suicide. The next day over coffee, I asked him to be the first president of Hemlock. "Why me?" he exclaimed. To which I replied: "You're the only person available!" I appointed myself executive director, Richard Scott was our legal adviser, and Ann served as treasurer of this miniature group. (Scott was also a physician but preferred law.)

On August 12, 1980, I booked the hall of the Los Angeles Press Club, where press conferences are held, to announce the arrival of the Hemlock Society. Larue and I mounted the podium before the assembled reporters and cameramen, but Dr. Scott and Ann stood at the back, still nervous about how things would go, positioned to beat a hasty retreat if things got embarrassing. Larue and I had no such fears. Coincidentally, less than an hour before the press conference started, a woman who had heard about the new organization approached me with a request to join. So I signed up Shirley Carroll O'Connor, who remained a member for at least the next twenty-five years and was still working as a volunteer for Compassion and Choices at age ninety.

After outlining Hemlock's mission to the reporters, I was asked by one: "How big are you?" to which I replied, truthfully due to Shirley O'Connor but somewhat evasively, "We're growing every day." Luckily no journalist followed up with the question as to how much growth, which would have revealed a mere four officers and one member! Another journalist asked if Hemlock was going to be in the yellow pages. "Of course," I answered. "There will be nothing covert or secret about this organization."

As a result of the press conference, we received hundreds of letters from people expressing interest. Only two were hostile, predicting that we were to be consigned to some special region of hell where we would meet an ugly end. The publisher of the paperback *Jean's Way* in London had an excess of stock and offered me some free, provided I did not sell them in England. To his surprise, I accepted five thousand copies, for he did not know that I was about to ship my furniture to Santa Monica, and there was ample space for these books. We disposed of them all fairly quickly to the new Hemlock supporters for a donation of four dollars. Having literature immediately available to our members made a big impression on them. Now, nearly thirty years later, many people remind me that they were charter members in those heady days.

It cannot be said that I rushed into the Hemlock project, with all the work and controversy it entailed, for five years had passed since Jean's death.

BUILDING HEMLOCK

Every person who had ever contacted me on this issue, plus the five hundred American names and addresses passed on by the London organization, was now contacted by mail, and membership topped the one-thousand mark within a few months. What the members most wanted, I now set out to provide: a book on how to end one's life with the use of drugs. Richard Scott, lawyer and physician—who joined Hemlock's board of directors once he had realized that its public reception was without problems— advised me to get true accounts of terminally ill people's own suicides and report them in great detail in a book. His advice was that, in the US, a writer could not be sued or prosecuted for telling the truth. Within the stories, the exact quantities of drugs ingested and the consequences would be given.

Hemlock appealed to all its members for personal stories of helping another to die. The response was huge, and soon I had all the material needed to write *Let Me Die Before I Wake*, at which point in 1981 I ran out of money. Traveling around the US at my own expense to interview people was expensive. Up until then, I had been financing Hemlock and myself with the royalties from *Jean's Way*, but these were now winding down. I had resigned from the *Los Angeles Times* to start Hemlock, and then the *London Sunday Times* understandably canceled my retainer fee when I declined to report on an aircraft disaster in the Antarctic because I was due to be the principal speaker at the first Hemlock public meeting. I had to make Hemlock work or abandon it and return to journalism. Simultaneously, not a few journalistic colleagues dropped me. It seems I had offended the Fourth Estate journalistic canon that a writer does not get involved in something she or he has written about, not to mention campaign on a taboo subject like assisted suicide. On a friendly visit back to the *Sunday Times* newsroom, one journalist taunted me: "I see you've started a new religion, Derek." I heard that another old acquaintance on a different newspaper had asserted publicly that I had gone "totally mad." No more commissions for articles reached me, except on the subject of right to die. Books about the *Sunday Times* somehow managed to avoid including my name. But I was not bothered by this exclusion; advancing Hemlock's cause was far more interesting and spiritually rewarding.

A letter was sent to all Hemlock members—by now totaling some three thousand—telling them that the "how-to" book was in manuscript form, but there was no financing available to pay for its printing. Members were asked to order and pay in advance, which was a pretty unusual request. Yet about two thousand members trusted this offer, and soon Hemlock had enough cash to print the book and mail it out to the subscribers. *Let Me Die Before I Wake*, constantly updated and revised, continued to bring Hemlock a steady cash flow for the next ten years. When it first appeared in 1981, Hemlock, out of caution, confined the book to members only, but there were protests from some in the book trade that this was "not the American way." At the start of 1982, the book was thrown open to sale in stores and libraries. The book attracted almost no attention in the media, which at that time did not take the issue of assisted dying seriously. But right to die supporters for the next ten years bought *Let Me Die Before I Wake* at the rate of approximately twenty-five thousand copies a year. The CBS TV current affairs program *60 Minutes* in 1985 called it "the bible of euthanasia." This was the second time this program had developed a segment related to hastened deaths. The first in 1980 had centered on Jean and me, but five years later the approach to the subject now was broader. The second segment featured people living in Arizona going over the border into Mexico to purchase lethal drugs, cheaply and legally, and taking them home to hide in shoe boxes or clothes closets. I was not on the show; my only part in it was that travelers were seen showing my "how-to" book to pharmacists in Mexico and asking for the drugs listed there.

Not wanting to be categorized as an organization with only a "suicide manual" to offer, Hemlock was quick to publish other books on the subject, notably reprints of *Jean's Way* and Doris Portwood's classic *Common Sense Suicide*, which introduced the idea of "balance sheet suicide" for the elderly. Mrs. Portwood argued that there might be a stage in an aged person's life when the combination of failing health and advanced years might justify deliberately drawing it to a close as a personal choice. Hemlock also commissioned Dr. Larue to write *Euthanasia and Religion* (Grove Press, 1985), which sold widely to colleges and libraries. A paperback original, it was the first easy-to-read description of how the religions in the world viewed suicide, assisted suicide, and euthanasia.

Publishing books on the right to die issue was looked upon with disfavor, as inevitable money losers, by the publishing industry until Betty Rollin's gripping story of helping her mother to die, *Last Wish* (Simon & Schuster, 1985), became a *New York Times* best seller. This sales breakthrough persuaded Harper & Row, a major New York publisher (now HarperCollins), to commission me to write a full-length history of euthanasia, *The Right to Die* (1986). Unable to complete it myself within the nine months specified by the publisher, my wife Ann Wickett, who was a skilled researcher and writer—plus two more research-ers—were brought into the project. Ann produced some of the finest chapters. At that point in time, access to background, stud-ies, and general information on the right to die was limited. It needed to be dug out of university archives, libraries, and old newspaper files—a contrast to the mid-1990s when there was a glut of instant information on the Internet, plus a plethora of articles and books on the once taboo subject.

A by-product of this book's commission was that the royal-ties earned (some forty thousand dollars) enabled Hemlock per-manently to expand its library and research services. *The Right to Die* was also published in Britain, and in translation in Spain and Germany, which together with the international acceptance of *Jean's Way* (five translations) started to give Hemlock its world reputation. Nevertheless, the membership was confined to the United States. When foreigners sought to join Hemlock, we encouraged them to join their local group or form one of their own.

Throughout the 1980s, when right to die was a low-priority public policy issue, Hemlock organized national conferences that attracted considerable public and media attention. The first chapter was set up in Tucson, Arizona, in 1983, when I was asked to speak at the City Center YWCA. I arrived expecting an audi-ence of twenty but found to my astonishment that it numbered 120. A vibrant chapter was immediately set up and flourishes to this day. It was followed by eighty more chapters by 1990. My modus operandi in forming chapters was to go to a city after writing to all the local members that I would be speaking at a certain place at a specified time. Then I would also inform the media of the meeting and that the intention was to set up a local Hemlock chapter. It almost always worked. Those who turned up to the meeting—sometimes several hundred, more often a dozen or so—would be encouraged to begin their own chapter. We had a handbook containing guidance on how to do it.

Gradually Hemlock came to be widely known, even if not always accepted, in the US. It had loyal supporters and fervent enemies.

My main avenue for securing visibility for the cause was talk radio. I employed a Hollywood radio publicist, Irwin Zucker, to get me on shows. In a busy year, I talked on as many as three hundred shows, at the end of each program giving out Hemlock's address and telephone number. It was a fruitful partnership with Zucker. Talk-show hosts discovered that the right to die topic attracted plenty of listeners and abundant call-ins, because everybody had a view on the matter, or a horror story to tell of a loved one's death. I averaged about twenty-five television shows, local and national, in a year, and two hundred to three hundred radios shows, which probably would not have occurred without my books as the entrée.

In 1985, as public acceptance grew larger, the organization grew bolder and started publishing drug charts in its newsletter, *Hemlock Quarterly*, and then distributing reprints for two dollars to all who wrote and asked. The membership, only some 3 percent of whom were terminally ill, was always hungry for information on lethal drugs and how to get them. The newsletter catered to this demand whenever possible. How many terminally ill people ended their lives with the information in *Let Me Die*

Before I Wake and the newsletter will never be known, although I estimate that it must be in the low thousands over a period of ten years. Once the self-deliverance has occurred, the family naturally retreats into a shell, rarely telling even me what happened.

By 1987, Hemlock's membership totaled fifteen thousand; within another two years it had doubled. The reason for the spurt in growth was the attempt to qualify a ballot initiative in California in 1988, which, if it had passed, would have legalized voluntary euthanasia and physician-assisted suicide for terminally ill adults. The attempt failed miserably in terms of signatures gathered because Hemlock and its then political arm, Americans for Death with Dignity, lacked the money to finance the paid signature-gathering essential in such a huge state as California, where some four hundred thousand signatures are required to get on the ballot. Our volunteers strove mightily on the streets and in the shopping malls but could not get enough signatures to qualify. Still, the publicity surrounding the attempt—particularly the critical attention given to the wording of the first such model law ever published—was so useful and effective that supporters who had not been aware of Hemlock came forward in droves.

It puzzled Hemlock's staff and leadership that we were never able to get famous people to support our cause—either by having their names on our letterhead, being keynote speakers at our conferences, or giving money. We had Hollywood just on the other side of town! On one occasion, a California newspaper carried a long interview with the actor George C. Scott in which he said he had seen several colleagues die badly, so he favored assisted suicide. I wrote to him, care of his agent, and as diplomatically as possible asked if he would support Hemlock in some way. I was careful not to ask for money. There was no reply. In 1985, Katharine Hepburn made a film that was a black comedy about euthanasia—*The Ultimate Solution of Grace Quigley*, in which a senior citizen's group employs a hit man to kill them in the street without their suspecting it. I wrote to Ms. Hepburn asking if she would speak at one of our conferences, and at first she said she would. Then she wrote again, saying she had changed her mind. She gave us no further support, although it has been revealed in a recent biography that she kept not one, but two copies of *Final Exit* in her bedroom, and presented copies to her friends.

Academics of huge standing, such as the behavior psychologist B. F. Skinner, the psychiatrist Bruno Bettelheim, and the theologian Joseph F. Fletcher, were charter members of Hemlock, but their names did not carry much weight with the public. (Skinner and Fletcher died naturally; Bettelheim took his life.) Perhaps Hemlock's most famous supporter was the science-fiction writer Isaac Asimov, who allowed me to reproduce in the *Hemlock Quarterly* an article of his on euthanasia at no charge. He wrote me that he would be a speaker at our conferences, but he was unable to travel, and we held none in New York. Asimov's greatest contribution to the cause was his spontaneous endorsement of *Final Exit* in which he said the following:

> No decent human being would allow an animal to suffer without putting it out of his misery. It is only to human beings that human beings are so cruel as to allow them to live on in pain, in hopelessness, in living death, without moving a muscle to help them. It is against such attitudes that this book fights.

Try as we might, even with our nearby show-business contacts, Hemlock never persuaded any actor or actress to lend a name in support. Probably most of our requests never got past their theatrical agents or publicity managers, who instinctively want to protect their clients from controversy, and certainly not death

and dying! It is not unknown in the United States for show business people to support a political party or a cause of social concern, but it is fairly rare. In the case of euthanasia, it is totally
absent in the US, but curiously, not so in Britain, where famous
artists such as Dirk Bogarde, Zoe Wannamaker, Rosalie Crutch-
ley, Ludovic Kennedy, Jonathan Miller, and Tom Conti allowed
their reputations and skills to be used to advance the cause. This
dichotomy has always puzzled me.

What sort of person is attracted to an organization devoted to
the depressing subject of dying? A survey of Hemlock members
in 1995 found that only 7 percent were terminally ill, knocking
out the myth that only dying people joined the group. The memberships' feelings on religion are perhaps the most interesting.
The survey found that 35.5 percent had no religion, 31.1 percent were Protestant, 12.6 percent were Jewish, Roman Cath-
olics were 3.5 percent, and those who said that they believed in
a non-mainstream religion made up 17.2 percent. Here are the
survey's overall conclusions:

> Hemlockers are older, married, Caucasian, predominantly
> female with grown children . . . highly educated, finan-
> cially stable homeowners, politically active and informed,
> and tend to be "slightly left of center" . . . both mentally
> and physically healthy and concerned with investigating
> future health-related life options . . . interested in fighting
> to preserve their right to individual self-determination in
> terms of right to die. ("Who's Fighting to Die, A Look at
> Hemlock Society Membership," by Jeffrey J Kamakahi,
> PhD, and Elaine Fox, PhD, in *Timelines*, July 1996.)

As the 1990s approached, Hemlock had grown into an influen-
tial organization and could no longer be run from the house it

occupied. Larger and more suitable premises were required than the organization could afford in Los Angeles. A library was an essential requisite, as the subject was becoming more popular with scholars and writers. Tiring of Southern California after ten years, I decided to move Hemlock to Eugene, Oregon, where costs would be lower and the quality of life for myself and Ann would be better. With the board's agreement, Hemlock was expanded in its new headquarters, and the growth continued unabated.

Gerald Larue had been consistently reelected president of Hemlock, but when the organization moved to Oregon in 1988, he felt it was time to step down. The board of directors rewarded his years of dedicated service by electing him "president emeritus." Larue had left me pretty much alone to run Hemlock, but never failed to turn up to chair the monthly board meetings where serious policy decisions were made. His academic prestige, powerful charismatic presence, brilliant public speaking ability, and gracious personal manner had provided a significant boost to Hemlock's growth over the years. It was support of that quality from him and others that convinced me to carry on with Hemlock's goals.

Now the World

The same year that Hemlock was founded, I played a part in founding the World Federation of Right to Die Societies. It was the Japanese who first floated the idea that right to die groups around the globe would benefit from getting together frequently to discuss their problems and exchange ideas. The gynecologist Dr. Tenrei Ota, famous for inventing a birth-control diaphragm, called the first meeting in Tokyo in 1976. It was attended by six organizations, chiefly from the United States, the United Kingdom, and Australia. (I had not, at that point, entered the movement.) There was another meeting in San Francisco two years later, which I attended and spoke to an audience about Jean's manner of death. As the 1980 conference loomed in Oxford, England, Sidney Rosoff and I put our heads together on ways to solidify the movement with an agreed name, a constitution, and elected officers. It was the only way it was likely to raise money and enroll more organizations. Sidney, a New York tax attorney who doubled as chairman of the Society for the Right to Die, drafted the constitution, which the Oxford conference accepted after some amendments. In the teeth of opposition groups that wanted to call the organization a "council," I argued successfully that the word "federation" was more appropriate because in no way was it a governing body, which the word "council" implied. At the dinner in the historic and imposing University Hall of the ancient university, Dr. Ota amused everyone by handing out complimentary copies of the Ota Ring diaphragm he had invented. The next day, Sidney Rosoff was elected the World Federation's first president, with me as newsletter editor, a post which I held on and off for the next twenty years. When I first ran for president, I was defeated by an 11–10 vote because some of the old guard at the time considered that Hemlock was too progressive. The next time around, I was unanimously elected president for 1988–90.

By the time of the 2006 conference in Toronto, there were 230 delegates from 55 organizations around the world. With this enormous growth in interest in choice in dying, the Netherlands and Belgium have, since 2003, legalized voluntary euthanasia and physician-assisted suicide. The Swiss have had non-physician-assisted suicide—even for foreigners—since 1942, and the state of Oregon legalized it for residents only in 1997.

MURDER CHARGE

The only trial of a Hemlock member accused of murder occurred in 1990 while I had taken a sabbatical leave to write *Final Exit*. I dropped my writing and flew to Detroit to arrange for the defense of Robert Harper on a first-degree murder charge for putting a plastic bag over his wife's head at her request. Not only were the Harpers long-time Hemlock members, but something he had read in *Hemlock Quarterly* had convinced him that in Michigan there was no law against assisting a suicide, which was true then. But Mr. Harper missed our warning that a state that has no prohibition might instead charge a person with manslaughter or murder. The Harpers flew to Detroit thinking to take advantage of the absence of an assisted-suicide law. After his wife's chosen way of accelerated death—she had advanced cancer—Mr. Harper innocently told the police what he had done. The result was a murder charge.

Mr. Harper, aged seventy-two, refused a plea bargain that would have given him probation for manslaughter, insisting he had done the right thing for his wife. So I set about getting him the best defense lawyers in the area, settling on a law firm that dealt almost every day in murders and other serious crimes. Hemlock members in the Detroit area criticized me for employing a firm that was infamous for defending the worst type of criminals, but my instincts told me that experienced lawyers like that would be more likely to get Mr. Harper off. They also agreed to a low fee for their services; on the first day of the trial I discovered why. Walking down the court corridors with one of the defense attorneys, I noticed that people were constantly saying to him: "Welcome back." So I asked the attorney where he had been. "In prison," he replied. I was a bit shaken until he explained: "Tax evasion." Being part of our high-visibility case with a human touch to it went part of the way toward rehabilitating him in court work.

The defense did a good job of defending Mr. Harper, with another lawyer attracting a lot of humorous attention by parading around the court, and speaking to the jury with a plastic bag over his head. Plenty of documentary evidence was supplied that demonstrated that Mrs. Harper planned this form of death. I gave evidence about the way the article in *Hemlock Quarterly* was open to misunderstanding because it was true that Michigan at the time had no prohibition—though it eventually did, as a response to Dr. Kevorkian's actions in the same period. Just before the jury went out to consider its decision, in a desperate move to get a conviction, the prosecution reduced the charge from first-degree to second-degree murder. The jury would have none of it and acquitted Mr. Harper completely. Hemlock's membership paid the defense costs of fourteen thousand dollars through a special fund. For me, this type of case was one of the chief reasons I had formed Hemlock.

PRESTIGIOUS SUPPORT

Hemlock was fortunate to have during its first eleven years the wisdom and guidance of the philosopher known as "the father of biomedical ethics." I first met Dr. Joseph F. Fletcher at the Oxford Right to Die Conference. His greatest fame came from his 1960 book *Situation Ethics*, in which he was the first philosopher to argue that some situations are so serious, so life threatening, that one has to perform unusual acts; shooting a person who is burning to death is one standard example. He argued that one did not always have to obey traditional and religious rules but "do the loving thing." Fletcher had already predicted in his

1950 book *Morals and Medicine* the coming fight in America over abortion and euthanasia because of high-tech medicine's arrival. In Oxford, I asked Fletcher if he would become a leader of Hemlock. "If I was forty years younger I would join you fellows," he responded. He also wanted to remain loyal to the Society for the Right to Die, which he helped found and had served as past president. Nevertheless, Fletcher was a firm supporter of Hemlock, as well as being a valuable advisor to me when I had difficulties. He also contributed articles to *Hemlock Quarterly* and introductions to books and pamphlets. Fletcher died in 1991 at age eighty-five.

Chapter 12

A HORRIBLE YEAR

TROUBLES COME IN PATCHES. The worst year in my life was 1986. A person doesn't look for personal issues of dying and death, but sometimes they come in a bundle. At the end of that year, an Australian television journalist interviewing me said, "Derek, you seem to be surrounded by death."

To which I replied, "It can happen to us all. It will probably happen to you one day, too." Although I was heavily involved in the movement for the right to choose to die, I did not go looking for cases.

My elder brother Garth had spent most of his working life in the open air, first as a farm laborer, secondly as a car salesman. The English damp had given him painful ear problems for which he sought medical help. He was advised to have a grommet inserted in his eustachian tube between nose and ear. This would stop the drainage into the ear that was causing infection. Told that the procedure could not be done on Britain's national health system for many months, Garth opted for private surgery. He checked into a small Chesterfield clinic in the morning and was scheduled for release later that day. Little did he or anyone else think that this would be his last day at the age of fifty-eight. Inserting the grommet was a small but extremely sensitive procedure, so he was given anesthesia; before the surgeons could even begin their work, the anesthesia had killed him. The two doctors struggled to revive him, but after four minutes his brain was damaged beyond repair or recovery. Ironically, if Garth had been operated on in the Bristol Royal Infirmary, to which the two doctors were attached, the heart-lung machines there, designed to save patients with cardiac arrest, might have saved him. The private clinic had no such life-saving equipment. After thirty minutes of trying to revive him, he was rushed to the infirmary—too late—and put on life-support equipment in the intensive care ward. There he lay, a perfectly fit body without a functioning brain.

Alerted by a phone call from his wife, Louise, with the advantage of the eight-hour time difference, I managed to hop the last aircraft of the day out of Los Angeles for England. As I got to his bedside it chanced that a nurse was opening his eyes and shining a light into them. Garth's eyes were blank, the pupils motionless. I knew then that he was as good as dead. A doctor explained: "His brain is severely damaged; there is still some semblance of life in the cortex."

Like the rest of the family, I was shocked and furious that Garth had died undergoing such a minor medical procedure. I determined to find out what had gone wrong. To put pressure on the medical people, I immediately informed the local newspapers, threatening to bring a lawsuit unless there was a satisfactory explanation. Garth had been a successful businessman and a local magistrate, so they took notice. Although the hospital automatically carried out its own autopsy, I ordered a second, independent one, for which the family paid.

Among ourselves in the family we debated whether it was appropriate to have the life-support equipment turned off and let what was left of poor Garth expire naturally. His wife, Louise, was an experienced nurse, rising to the rank of hospital matron before retiring. Thus she was fully aware of the seriousness of the situation. One of his daughters was on her way from her home in Australia, and we thought it best to wait for her to see the state of her father before coming to any group decision. On a Sunday afternoon, we all met—his wife, two sons, three daughters, and me—in a sad family gathering at Garth's house. We realized that Garth would never wake up. After a couple of hours of talking and numerous cups of tea, there was agreement that I should go to the hospital the next day and ask for Garth to be disconnected and allowed to die. Immediately after the decision was made, the two younger daughters, Joanne and Claire, burst into tears and fled to a bedroom. The rest of us sat stunned. But after about half an hour, the two young women came back to the table and said bravely, "We agree that Father should be allowed to die."

As the senior person in the Humphry family, it fell to me to go to the hospital. In the intensive care ward, I took one last look at Garth. What struck me most was that everybody I could see in that ward—they had only towels over their private parts—appeared emaciated and at death's door. By contrast, Garth looked physically fit and well, slightly overweight, and breathing through a machine. When the doctor in charge came up to me, I told her, "The family has decided that we accept Garth is brain-dead, so we would like all the equipment switched off and let him go."

She replied, "Mr. Humphry, we were only waiting for you to ask."

I watched as all the equipment and tubes were removed and Garth was wheeled into a private room where the family could gather. Four hours later, on April 14, 1986, the last vestiges of his life faded.

Garth's death affected me deeply in two ways. First, why had it happened that a fit, middle-aged person going for outpatient surgery in these modern-medicine times could die before a minor procedure had even begun? And at a point when he had found a happy marriage and was at last prospering as a Ford motorcar dealer. Second, the person who had in my childhood been, in effect, both my acting mother and my father was robbed of his life. He had been so important to me. I still cherished him, even though we now lived separate lives thousands of miles apart. (Father never knew about this tragedy, having died three years earlier, while Mother of course was totally out of touch.)

In England, all sudden deaths must be followed by an inquest, which is a court hearing with the coroner (a lawyer who acts as a sort of judge) and a jury. The two doctors attending Garth gave evidence of their administering the anesthetics fentanyl, thiopentone, and atracurium besilate. They said that Garth had given permission for such drugs to be used. What followed was that one of the drugs—probably the thiopentone—had given Garth an anaphylactic shock and he died instantly of a heart attack.

The lawyer representing the family asked why Garth was given thiopentone when it was known to be risky with patients with asthma. Why did they not test Garth for reaction to the drug in advance? The doctors responded that Garth's asthma was during his childhood, thus they did not think it relevant to a middle-aged man who no longer showed asthmatic symptoms. Because I had been making such a stink about the case in the newspapers, the coroner shrewdly called me to give evidence, so as to let off family steam, so to speak. But there was little of importance I could tell the court, other than that Garth was in all respects a healthy, golf-playing individual who worked hard. The coroner ruled that "The precise cause of death" was as follows:

a. Acute bronchopneumonia;

b. Hypoxic cerebral damage;

c. Acute anaphylaxis secondary to general anesthesia (with fentanyl, thiopentone, and atracurium).

The family commenced a lawsuit against the doctors and the hospital because evidence from the private autopsy showed disturbing damage to vital internal organs, indicating that perhaps something else had gone wrong. But no doctor would back us up, and we dropped the case for lack of corroborating evidence. For the prior ten years, I had been writing about and lecturing people to get second opinions, sign living wills, and get informed on assisted suicide in case those problems should arise, and now I was getting painful experience of my own on disconnecting life support. Later that year, I published my first hardcover book (coauthored with Ann Wickett) entitled *The Right to Die: Understanding Euthanasia* (Hemlock Society, 1991). It was separately published in the United States, Germany, Britain, and Spain. In the London edition I added a new dedication: "For Garth (1927–1986), whose untimely death showed that modern medical technology can take away life as well as save it."

Breaking Up

There were other troubles ahead. My marriage to Ann Wickett had been experiencing difficulties for several years. I had only myself to blame. She was "drop-dead beautiful" (as Americans love to say), extremely bright (BA from Boston University, MA from Toronto University), and the younger daughter of a Boston banker, Arthur Kooman, and his wife, Ruth, of Belmont, Massachusetts.

After Jean died, still in England among my circle of friends and office colleagues, I had not come across any woman whom I felt like marrying after Jean died, so I resorted to the "personals" advertisements in literary weekly journals where men and women speak glowingly of themselves in search of love mates. I dated two or three, but even there I drew a blank.

Then I saw an advertisement in the *New Statesman* which read: "Attractive blond, piquant, 33, about to be divorced, PhD student (but not at all heavy into academia), seeks compatible male, 35 or older, interesting, keen mind, good sense of humor, type to put his feet up on the furniture. Objective? Friendship, camaraderie, or more if chemistry so encourages. Box 1240."

I replied because the tone of the ad struck me as out of the ordinary. About a week later, I received a long letter with a photograph from a student at the Shakespeare Institute, a branch of Birmingham University. She wrote that she would shortly be spending a week at the British Museum in London, working on her thesis, and we might meet. It turned out that she was also meeting other men who had responded. We met at the YWCA where she was staying, had a drink in a pub in Covent Garden, linked up a couple of times more, and we were in love. Within weeks we were living together in my basement apartment in Kentish Town, north London, and in 1976 we were wed in a civil ceremony.

I married Ann on the classic rebound from a great twenty-two-year marriage to Jean. Within the first year of our marriage, Ann's problems began to show up: raging tempers resulting in anything near to hand being thrown at me; terrible fear of abandonment even if I was staying away one night on journalistic business; agoraphobia, fear of flying, and fearsome jealousy. For example, once when I went to dinner with the well-known writer Germaine Greer (it was an interview, not a social engagement),

Ann punched out our bedroom window in anger. From the moment they met, Ann hated my children, and they reciprocated. I considered a divorce in the first year. Perhaps I should have thrown myself on the understanding of friends and family, admitting that on the rebound I had made a terrible, hasty mistake. It was entirely my fault, for I had proposed marriage to Ann, not the other way around.

Four things checked me from immediate divorce:

1. My childhood was peppered with other people's quarrels and divorces. Now I had joined the pack.
2. Was I giving up too easily?
3. My ignorance of psychological conditions. Perhaps Ann would get better; she wanted to.
4. As a woman and as a person when in a placid mental state, I loved her very much.

It began to strike me more forcibly that she was mentally ill when she would angrily point her finger at me and declare, "Don't you ever say I'm ill!" This despite the fact that during and after her first marriage in Toronto she had twice attempted suicide, had spent six months in the psychiatric ward of Toronto General Hospital, and continued to be under the care of a psychiatrist or a psychologist. Several times when we were first in Los Angeles, I found her in a catatonic state and took her to hospital. It was usually drug related.

I had asked her for a divorce in 1984 following a colossal row. She had argued for around eighteen hours a day for three wearying weeks that I must dismiss two Hemlock directors who had criticized her. My response that I could not and would not dismiss them fell on deaf ears. I told her that they would sue if they were asked to step down on such flimsy grounds. This incessant clamoring for their unfair dismissal merely because they had criticized her—politely and justifiably, in my presence—brought me to the point that I asked for a divorce. This shook Ann. She opposed the breakup so hysterically, including issuing threats to smash the Hemlock Society, that I caved in and carried on. Now in 1986, her mood swings were becoming worse, her foot-stamping anger fits more frequent, and I was at the end of my tether. When calm and balanced, Ann could be a loving, delightful person, generous to her friends, a shrewd and welcome advisor to me on literary matters. When moody and angry, Ann was a liar, was bitter to her friends and my children, and made vicious and unnecessary comments about her parents. "I wish they were dead," she would yell. She wrote them many horrible letters—which I later saw—accusing them of not appreciating what a lovely, talented daughter they had. However, I found Ruth and Arthur Kooman, both university graduates, to be a nice, suburban, elderly people who over the years had been most generous and tolerant in support of Ann. Perhaps they had made mistakes in her upbringing, but then don't we all sometimes make tactical blunders in raising a family?

My three children never phoned home for the fourteen years we were married for fear of getting a diatribe from Ann about their "selfishness." They phoned me at the office when necessary. I censored myself from ever mentioning, even in the most harmless way, that I had a family, as that only triggered a blazing row.

Ann would have close girlfriends one day—yet a few days later they were her enemies. Ours was a stormy marriage, although we largely hid this from our family and friends. From 1984 onward I regarded the marriage to be no longer one of love and trust, and to be over. I was hanging on, largely for the sake of the Hemlock Society, which was going from strength to strength. We both had affairs with other people, hopefully keeping them secret. The love of another woman who was emotionally balanced made my home life bearable. At Ann's insistence, we went to marriage counseling sessions. I remember one where the therapist tried hard to persuade Ann to put behind her the dispute with my children (now young men), but she could not manage that. Usually Ann's anger exploded at the end of dinner, after she had consumed two or three drinks. Alcohol was invariably the trigger.

Another reason I remained in the marriage was that this was the year my first hardcover book in the US was to be published. A brilliant researcher, Ann wrote some of the finest chapters in the book. Her research into erudite subjects was retold in the smoothest prose. My half of the book was based mainly on experience, observation, and reflection. During that summer came the time to launch the book. For every waking minute of three days, Ann fought me to have her name on the book cover as the lead author, instead of "by Derek Humphry and Ann Wickett." Her demands became so antagonistic that I stopped the car at a roadside telephone and called the publisher in New York. "Do that and we'll cancel the contract," he said. That shut Ann up.

With the success of Betty Rollin's book *Last Wish* had shown, Harper & Row (now HarperCollins) realized that the right to die issue was becoming hugely controversial in the public mind. Therefore, it planned two big book-promotion tours, with Ann along the West Coast and me touring the East Coast.

Ann visited Los Angeles, San Francisco, and Seattle and many places in between talking up our book. I toured Pittsburgh, Baltimore, Philadelphia, and Washington, DC, doing as many as ten talk shows a day, until I reached New York. I thought the promotion was going fine, but it wasn't. The chief editor at Harper & Row called me to his office for a stunning criticism. The company had received numerous complaints from television and radio producers on the West Coast that Ann was rude and uncooperative; some shows were spoiled, he said. The company had put up a lot of money for a big promotional tour but had never come across this situation before. I was flabbergasted. And as a professional journalist and communicator, it hurt too. All I could think of to explain this behavior was to say that Ann's elderly parents were terribly ill and at the point of death. This must be unbalancing her, I told the chief. I promised to do my best to make amends. I kept to myself the information that, addicted to Valium, when coming down from a high, Ann could be the meanest person you ever met. I think this was the root cause of the book-promotion tour troubles. She probably had taken lots of Valium overnight to steel her nerves for the grueling round of TV and radio talk shows next day.

When I got back from New York, I did not tell her of this debacle. I knew she would deny it was her fault, blaming others for their stupidity. She could never bear to be criticized, no matter how tactfully it was put. Somebody else was always to blame.

Double Exit

Soon we were in another critical situation. Ann and her elder sister, Jane Kooman Canfield, had quarreled in their teens and in the following thirty-odd years had never spoken. On the rare occasions when they needed to communicate, they used me to transmit a message. I got word from Jane that both Mr. and Mrs. Kooman were so ill and debilitated that they could no longer live alone. They must go into a nursing home. Their doctor insisted that the home healthcare they were getting was not enough. Arthur was ninety-two with congestive heart failure and a painful back; Ruth, at seventy-seven, had suffered several strokes, leaving her so handicapped that it took her ten minutes to cross the living room with the aid of a walker. Over the telephone between Boston and Santa Monica, both her parents told Ann and me that they wanted to commit suicide together rather than go into care. Given their ages and their illnesses, it was hard to argue against that idea. Plus, they had always chosen to be members of the Hemlock Society. Fortunately, as her parents aged and deteriorated, Ann had become more loving and understanding of them. Now they were asking the ultimate act of love: help us to die.

Bad news also came from England that my elder son's marriage had broken up, and there were lots of legal and money problems. Edgar and Vivienne had married too young, too quickly, and the marriage was doomed from the start, in my opinion.

For once, Ann and I agreed on something. We would help her parents to die if that was really what they wished. I secured through the mail several hundred Vesperax pills (secobarbital plus brallobarbital) from a legal source I knew in Switzerland. (Somebody talked too much about this source, so it later closed.) We flew to Boston and spent some time with Arthur and Ruth, going over their reasons for killing themselves. I was present, too, when the couple told their family doctor that they intended to die on Sunday. He did not seem surprised, tactfully saying nothing in response.

Arthur was calm and adamant that he wanted to die now, insisting that Ruth must decide for herself what to do. Ann and I promised to take her back to Santa Monica, put her in a good local nursing home, and see her every day. There was plenty of her own money available to pay for the best of care. Clearly Arthur was dying, but although she was very handicapped, and could expect another stroke, she was not terminal. Nevertheless, Ruth would not budge.

"No. I want to go with Arthur," she insisted again and again. When she and I were alone, I repeated the offer to take her to Santa Monica, but she would not waver.

I told the family that I would not be a party to this double suicide unless I knew the views of the other daughter, who had told me by telephone that she had washed her hands of her parents' care. A meeting was arranged in the dining room for the next morning—the day they were planning to die—and I explained the situation to Jane.

"Where do you stand on what your parents intend to do tonight?" I asked.

"I don't object, but I want nothing to do with it," Jane replied, and left.

Ann composed and typed out a suicide note for her parents, which they both, almost casually, signed. Two days later the *Boston Globe* reported their double suicide no differently from any normal obituary notice, with the usual summary of their life accomplishments and list of survivors. Without any flourish, the suicide note that the *Globe* in part reported (on July 23, 1986) said: "We have led full and fruitful lives, but now that we are in failing health we choose to die in a peaceful and dignified way."

And so we all ate a hearty early evening meal. On my advice, Arthur and Ruth ate more sparingly so as not to interfere with their forthcoming self-deliverance. A few drinks and toast. No one was maudlin or regretful. It was remarkably like a normal, Sunday evening dinner table in a middle-class Boston household.

Immediately after dinner, Ann put two hundred of the pills into the blending machine and crushed them up. A shower of dust blew up from the blender. Ann joked that this might cause her to be the first to go! Ann then mixed the lethal powder into two bowls, one containing applesauce, which Arthur had chosen, and the other in coffee ice cream, which Ruth enjoyed. The couple took several antiemetic pills so that they would not vomit.

Arthur and Ruth slept in separate rooms. After they had gone upstairs, using the handicapped stair lift chair that they had leased, Arthur went into his wife's bedroom and kissed her goodbye. At first, Ann wanted me to help her mother to die; I declined, saying that Arthur was my real friend and that a daughter should stick by her mother. There was no further discussion.

Sitting beside Arthur's bed, I asked him one more time if he was quite sure about ending his life. He was. I noted down what Arthur said: "I don't know how to thank you and Ann for what you are doing for us."

Then he eagerly scooped down the laced apple sauce, became woozy, and I said quite firmly, "Arthur! Say good-bye!" and he did. That seemed to be the closure I wanted. Within twenty minutes, he was dead. I assumed that the same thing was happening next door. Ann emerged onto the landing and said that her mother, too, was dead. (Several years later Ann claimed that she had also put a plastic bag over her mother's head. Because I was not in the room, I cannot deny it, but somehow I think this was a lie. Ruth had taken enough secobarbital to kill an ox. Ann did not mention it at the time or in her little book on the event, *Double Exit* [Hemlock Society, 1989.])

Our stormy marriage rumbled on for another three years until it exploded in a divorce war, as I shall relate later in this book.

Chapter 13

TO SEE YOURSELF

AS OTHERS SEE YOU

T O SEE ONESELF PORTRAYED onstage and screen is a strange experience. You feel disembodied, as though someone else has taken over your life, speaking your words. And you are totally in their hands, for better or worse.

The Theatre Royal, in Northampton, England, approached me for the rights to turn *Jean's Way* into a dramatic play. They couldn't afford to pay me anything at the beginning, so I had my New York literary agent, Robert Ducas, draw up a contract that allowed the Northampton Repertory Theatre to adapt the book and stage the play. If it transferred to the West End theater district or Broadway, then royalties would be paid. The actress and playwright Vilma Hollingbery wrote the play, to be directed by her husband Michael Napier Brown. They could not afford any noted actor, but did assemble a team of competent professionals.

They called the play *Is This the Day?* using Jean's first words on the morning of her death. Its world premiere was on May 10,

1990, and the review notices were promising. The well-known author and television presenter Ludovic Kennedy wrote in the *Guardian*: "A worthy dramatic interrogative to *Whose Life Is It Anyway?* . . . it is a long time since I sat in a theatre where attention to the play was so committed." (Kennedy was referring to the 1980s fictional hit play and movie about a quadriplegic asking to be allowed to die.)

"The most alertly, the most instinctively, artistic play of its genre," said the theatre critic of the *Independent on Sunday*.

"I very much doubt that I shall ever see a more brilliant, a more powerful, a more emotive, or a more real piece of theatre than *Is This the Day?*" wrote the critic of *The Stage*.

With these encomiums, the play looked to be on its way to a West End London production. Yet it was not to be. Scouts from the production companies had noted that, despite the praise, the audience was thin. The denial of death barrier had clicked in. I was unable to see it until the closing night. Of course, I would be the worst judge of the play, plus I was more involved in my emotional reactions to seeing Jean's and my story played by others onstage. What followed the fall of the curtain was more interesting: I, the playwright, the director, and some of the cast sat on the lip of the stage and engaged the audience in a debate far into the night about euthanasia and how this dramatic production had explored it.

Is This the Day? had several more short productions at repertory companies in Britain, Germany, and the United States but never really took off.

As a sidebar to this, however, Vilma Hollingbery was commissioned by Granada Television to rewrite it as a screen drama. A producer and director were appointed, and the casting began. It looked on course for a national viewing, but—not for the first time, as I will explain—the project crashed. The head of drama for Granada, Michael Cox, telephoned me to say he was leaving his job for a better one, and he doubted that his successor would continue with the play. It is customary, almost the rule, throughout show business that when appointed, a new head of drama will not take the responsibility for artistic choices made by a predecessor. Regardless of expense already incurred, they start again with their own ideas.

I'd gone through this before. When the book *Jean's Way* appeared in 1978, Columbia Pictures in Hollywood snapped up a film option, later bought the rights, proceeded to have three scripts written by a distinguished screenwriter at a cost of one hundred thousand dollars, and asked Lynn Redgrave to play the lead role. The person behind it was producer Sherry Lansing, who was very committed to the principles expounded in the story. She arranged for me to work with screenwriter Arnold Schulman, providing background. Ms. Lansing was one of the top producers in Hollywood at the time, having done *Kramer vs. Kramer*, *The China Syndrome*, *Fatal Attraction*, and other successful films. Nevertheless, I opened the *Los Angeles Times* one day in 1980 and saw the news that Ms. Lansing had been made the head of Paramount Studios, the first woman to hold such a position. Shortly afterwards, a note came from Columbia saying my film was dropped. The rights reverted to me after four years.

In a controversial subject like euthanasia, people can become deeply divided, mainly on religious grounds. I have my share of enemies—whom I prefer to call opponents. (I have never had threats on my life, nor have I received hate letters. Only once have I needed police protection to get me through a huge mob in order to speak at a public meeting in Melbourne, Florida, which is a stronghold of the Christian right.) Granada Television (which had already dropped the Hollingbery play) decided to mount another production about my life. They did so without asking my permission or letting me know and kept the production a close secret until news of it accidentally slipped out from a low-level employee. Its working title was *Hemlock* and eventually was shown with the title *Goodbye My Love*. Granada would not let me see the script. Instinctively I knew there was trouble here—it is an old trick not to let the subject of the article or play see the article or script so that they cannot sue to stop the launch of the production.

The television play, with the celebrated actor Robert Lindsay playing me, attracted only minimal attention. The television critic of *Country Life* described it thus: "It came over as fair, tentative and wooden, thus doing little or nothing to move the debate [on euthanasia] either forwards, backwards or even sideways." It later ran in the United States and Canada on cable channels and sank without a trace. When I viewed it, I was appalled at its naked bias against euthanasia; worse, it was full of factual errors that made me look a bad person. It implied that I had murdered Jean. Whole chunks of dialogue were ripped from my book, but—shrewdly—not enough for me to justify a copyright infringement. Even the title of the television docudrama was filched from Jean's last words.

Friends said that it looked as though I behaved like a monster. "Poisonous venom," declared a lady in Canada. For example, there was a shot of an empty barn and the voice-over said that I had taken the two farm tractors from Ann, thereby wrecking the farm. The truth was that I had taken the one tractor, which belonged to me, leaving hers behind. It was an easy-care hobby farm of twenty acres with a few horses and perhaps a dozen Highland cows, which are not milkers. There was a farm assistant permanently on call. Anyway, I had already handed my tractor over to her as part of the divorce settlement of goods and money between us. Another blunder was that the television movie came to a celebratory close with the victory of the Oregon Death With Dignity Act (1994, confirmed by ballot in 1997), giving me the entire credit for passing the law. This was embarrassing nonsense because although I had started the ball rolling nationally and in Oregon, it was a huge team effort to get physician-assisted suicide actually passed into law in this one American state.

I told the *London Daily Express* at the time: "I was astounded to see the cold, drab characterization of me by Robert Lindsay. To see somebody else assume your name, character and reputation, mouthing your own words—sometimes, inevitably, in a way you didn't intend—is difficult to stomach."

In the same *Express* interview, Lindsay told the writer that he thought I did not come out of the program well. "I got the feeling at one point that perhaps they were having a dig at Derek," he said (*London Daily Express*, January 4, 1997). I considered suing Granada. My lawyer in London, Ian Starr, said there was an actionable case, and he would, if I wanted, represent it. As an example that not all lawyers are grasping and greedy, he also advised me that I would be taking on a major media corporation that had a team of in-house lawyers who would fight all the way. Whatever the verdict, if the judge did not award me costs, I would be financially ruined. But I commend Ian for suggesting another plan of attack: England had a new Broadcasting Standards Commission set up by Parliament in 1996, which, as an alternative to a court of law, provides redress for members of the public who feel they have been treated or subjected to unwarranted infringement of privacy.

Therefore, I launched a complaint against Granada on the grounds that its researcher had misrepresented himself to me as working for a different program, for its failure to notify me about the program in advance and give me right of reply, and that the film insufficiently advised its viewers that the content was a mixture of fact and fiction. The Broadcasting Standard Commission, after a long investigation, upheld my complaint. Granada had to apologize to me both onscreen and in the legal columns of the *Times* newspaper.

Chapter 14

ENTER "FINAL EXIT"

T HROUGHOUT THE DECADE OF the 1990s, thanks to all its political activities, Hemlock's membership soared by some ten thousand to thirty-nine thousand, during which time I took a sabbatical summer to write a "how to" to replace the aging *Let Me Die Before I Wake*. When that book was written, ten years earlier, it had been extremely cautious in its approach to "self-deliverance" (a term I have tried to popularize in place of "suicide"). Now there was a much more enlightened attitude toward the terminally ill accelerating their ends with lethal drugs. In the planning stages were ballot initiatives in Washington State and California, which would need huge financial aid if they were to do better than the abortive initiative in California in 1988. I poured into the new book everything I had learned over the previous fifteen years, writing in a much more direct and instructive way this time. When finished, I entitled it *Final Exit: The Practicalities of Self-Deliverance and Assisted Suicide for the Dying*, little realizing how famous and successful it would become.

Final Exit was offered to numerous US publishers by my literary agent in New York, Robert Ducas, but all rejected it. It was the same story in Australia and Britain. Coincidentally, by the time this book was ready, Hemlock's other publications were being distributed to the book trade by Carol Publishing, a medium-large publishing house in New York. Steven Schragis, the owner, offered to publish *Final Exit*, but, to his astonishment, his staff refused to cooperate. Schragis was reluctant to defy his staff but treated the matter as a personal crusade. He offered to loan me the financing to publish it myself, so confident was he that he could recoup the money from his share of the sales. I politely declined, saying that Hemlock could afford to publish the book, and therefore if it succeeded, the organization deserved and needed the profits.

When it appeared in February 1991, only the Hemlock members realized its usefulness and snapped up a quarter of the forty thousand we had printed. Two hundred copies went out to reviewers, writers, and right to die experts, but after six months not a single paragraph had been printed about it. Many bookstores had it on their shelves without realizing what a ticking time bomb they were stocking. However, Schragis never lost faith in the book and pushed the New York media to take notice. None did. Then one day at a dinner party, he met Norman Pearlstein, then editor of the *Wall Street Journal*, and told him about this unusual book. The next day, Pearlstein asked writer Meg Cox to write an article for the "Marketplace" Friday column about the book. Cox tracked me down to my holiday spot in England and interviewed me on my reasons for writing such a strange book, also asking who in the US would hate *Final Exit*. I mentioned the Hastings Center and the National Right to Life Committee, among others, and as I had predicted, their spokespersons instinctively condemned the book. Susan Wolf, a lawyer and researcher at Hastings, told the *Journal*: "The troubling possibility is that people may get hold of this and kill themselves when they're in the throes of a reversible depression or some other state for which they could get help." Burke Balch, an official of Right to Life, described the book as "a loaded gun."

"Suicide Manual for Terminally Ill Stirs Heated Debate," the *Wall Street Journal*, "Marketplace," July 12, 1991. The newspaper article with this headline appeared on the second Friday in July. By Monday, the bookstores had been cleared out of *Final Exit*. Schragis called me from New York and asked for more copies. "Okay, I'll print another ten thousand," I replied.

"No, you don't understand," Schragis said. "I want another hundred thousand." I was staggered. The book sold like wildfire. People were lining up in bookstores when they opened for business to snap up the daily allocation. One writer joked, "Only in New York would people take a number and get in line to buy a book on how to commit suicide."

I was invited on to all the major serious television talk shows, and *Time* and *Newsweek* devoted pages to the book. In downtown Manhattan, a demonstration marched through the streets protesting its publication. New York's Cardinal Mahoney described it as "a new low in publishing." Canadian newspapers howled that it should not be allowed to cross their border, but the book trade there sold it by the tens of thousands. By August, it was on the *New York Times* best-seller list, where it remained for eighteen weeks. During September, *Publisher's Weekly* ranked it the best-selling nonfiction book in North America, while it finished up the fourth best-selling nonfiction book for the entire year. *US News & World Report* said: "As the author of a best-selling guide to suicide, Derek Humphry has placed himself at the center of a highly emotional moral debate" (September 30, 1991).

The book became the subject of satire and humor as well. *Saturday Night Live* did a sketch on the book's notoriety. The late night comedy shows reveled in it. In an August 1992 *Playboy* interview, I related the current fashion:

> *Playboy*: You must have stumbled across some good gallows humor. What's your favorite suicide joke?

> Humphry: My favorite is the one about the person who is just about to jump off the Brooklyn Bridge. A New York City policeman dashes up to him, aims a gun, and yells: "Get back or I'll shoot." The man gets back.
>
> Bob Hope, Jay Leno and Dave Letterman have joked about the book. Arsenio Hall did a sketch which was tremendous: people were calling up librarians, telling them that they wouldn't be bringing back their copy of *Final Exit*—they were going to use it. We don't mind being laughed at. You've arrived when you're part of the humor.

This line of humor developed because some Los Angeles newspapers had reported complaints from libraries that, with high public demand to borrow it, they had to keep ordering fresh copies of the book caused by its inevitable low rate of its return.

If ever there was an instance where the public's taste and the establishment's standards were in direct conflict, this was a classic. The more the churches, the ethicists, and right-wing columnists railed against the moral implications of the book, the more the public went out to buy it. Various Christian fundamentalist groups named me "Anti-Christ of the Month." It was the most talked about book in America in the fall of 1991: just how could a book on how to kill yourself become a number-one bestseller? What did this mean? Was America entering a period of nihilistic, suicidal behavior? Those few commentators who took the trouble to read the book saw that it was addressed, in a careful, responsible manner, only to the dying. And if people were buying, it then there was something wrong in the way we dealt with dying in America.

Final Exit was banned in Australia and New Zealand by censorship boards, but after an appeal we got it freed for sale provided it was shrink-wrapped and placed on a high shelf in bookstores. France has a 1986 law banning all literature that explains suicide. Immediately after *Final Exit* arrived in Paris in French translation (*Exit Final*), somebody placed a complaint with the government, which moved immediately to seize it. Fortunately, the publisher was tipped off that the gendarmes were on the way, so he loaded the entire stock onto a truck and rushed it over the border into Belgium. The *Times* of London reported that the book had been banned in Britain; it was wrong, and agreed to my request for a correction. The American Library Association included *Final Exit* in its list of "most challenged books" in lending libraries nationwide.

Hemlock grossed more than $2.2 million from book sales before they peaked at 550,000 hardcover copies. After printing, royalties, and commissions, Hemlock had a net of about $1.25 million, money that it was able to liberally pour into ballot initiatives to try and make assisted death no longer a crime. Over the years, Hemlock—the only "moneybags" in a movement made up mostly of elderly middle-class persons on pensions—gave this financial backing to state initiative campaigns: California 1988, $210,000; Washington 1991, $300,000; California 1992, $100,000; Oregon 1994, $205,000; Oregon 1997, $137,000; Maine 2000, $250,000. Total: $1,202,000. (These amounts were governed by the IRS tax laws.) Although the windfall of *Final Exit*'s huge earnings was its major revenue source, Hemlock also received thousands of small donations (totaling $109,000 in 1992), plus membership fees from its membership, then reaching an all-time high total of forty-five thousand.

Staggered by this startling and unexpected fame, I began to think that it was time to hand over the reins of Hemlock after twelve grueling years. Now sixty-two, I had no private pension because, until recently, Hemlock could not afford such a plan. Therefore, I quickly invested my royalties from the book and told Hemlock's directors that I was retiring in order to be a freelance writer and lecturer on death with dignity. "I believe in going when at the top, and when the organization is in excellent administrative and financial condition," I told the board. "I need a rest and a change. But I'm still with you in spirit."

Many of the board were glad to see me go because they were jealous of my reputation among the members and new public fame as an author. After almost a year of intensive research, a new executive director was appointed, but he did not fit in well with a board that was now determined to micromanage Hemlock. He resigned after two years. By 1997, Hemlock's membership had halved to around eighteen thousand, landing the new director, Faye Girsh, a sixty-two-year-old psychologist who had been the founder and president of the best Hemlock chapter, San Diego, with the uphill task of rebuilding the organization. This was at a time when other right to die groups were springing up to carry on the fight for law reform state by state. In my time as head of Hemlock, the group had a virtual monopoly on the theme of "physician-assisted suicide," but in 1993 there were nine other similar organizations, all vying for donations and memberships: Americans for Death with Dignity, Compassion in Dying, Death with Dignity Education Center, Friends of Dying Patients, Merian's Friends, and Dying Well Network (all of which dissolved by 2007), along with Euthanasia Research and Guidance

Organization (ERGO), Oregon Right to Die, and Oregon Death with Dignity Legal Defense and Education Center.

The majority of the workers in these organizations had been associated in one way or another—officer, employee, or member—with the Hemlock Society USA over the previous decade. What I had tentatively started in my Santa Monica garage in 1980 was now spawning a powerful and competitive movement for social and legal reform. Working alone, there was also the controversial Dr. Jack Kevorkian, who helped some 130 people to die in a transparent manner between 1990 and 1999 (see Chapter 18 for more).

Chapter 15

WHAT HAPPENED TO MOTHER?

I T IS STRANGE HOW my virtually nonexistent mother kept crop-
ping up in my life, loosely connected to the right to die movement. But then, my private life and my work, like it or not, have
always become interconnected. And that was how this part of my
life story went as well.

As I said earlier, Mother had left England for Australia with a
man other than my father when I was about three years old. I had
no memory of what she was like. She did not contact my brother
or me for the next twenty years. Out of the blue, she returned
with another husband and a son in 1953, hung around London
for a while, and returned three times to Australia and then back
again to England. Her long-suffering husband came the first
time and then sensibly refused to keep shuttling back and forth
on what was then a six-week voyage each way. I got on well with
Mother, although we did not get close, never had an intimate
conversation, and certainly never hugged. She visited Garth but
he was frosty, and his waspish wife was even curter. Being two

years older, Garth had witnessed and suffered through the kid-nappings and angry scenes that apparently marked the breakup of the marriage. I was too young to realize the pain of what was going on—I thought that was how life was for everybody! During her surprise reappearance, my father also saw her couple of times in London, and I gather the relationship was cordial. On our many pleasant outings, I played football with her eight-year-old son, Sean, in Hyde Park, London. It was a fairly good reunion all around. Yet there was a pervasive attitude of uncertainty.

When Mother announced that she was tired of London, cit-ing the drab weather compared to Australia's warmth, and that she would return to Australia with Sean for the very last time, I was not surprised. We had a friendly good-bye visit, and I prom-ised I would go out to Australia before long and visit her. I might join an Australian newspaper. She promised to let me know where she had settled with John. I assumed that the parting was felicitous, though because we did not love one another, it was not painful.

She lived another thirty years, but I never heard from her again.

As the years rolled by and I was fully occupied with raising a happy family and advancing in my journalistic career, I some-times wondered what had happened to her, but there was noth-ing I could do about it. Presumably she had returned to Australia, but to which part of that vast continent was not known to me. Garth said he didn't care. It was not so much that I cared but that I was puzzled. Why would she cut me off like that—twice? I'm the sort of person who likes to have answers, even if they are painful ones.

Jean's death in 1975 and the publication three years later of *Jean's Way* changed the situation. The book was so successful in Britain that it was also printed and published in Australia as a mass-market paperback. Therefore, the publisher invited me to tour Australia, appearing on television shows, radio talk programs, and newspaper interviews. My book was everywhere, even displayed on newspaper kiosks. Briefly, I was the most famous writer in Australia. I reckoned that mother, or her husband or son, would make contact, perhaps by calling the television or radio station. How could a mother of a son telling such a sad story of Jean's death not be moved to make contact? I considered it a certainty. But I was wrong.

When I was about to leave after two weeks of intense exposure through the media and public speaking, I was due to have an interview with a journalist from *Woman's Own* magazine, which possessed the biggest circulation in its field in Australia. I told the surprised reporter that really I was in Australia on a secret mission looking for my long-lost mother, but had failed hopelessly. The reporter was fascinated. I continued my book tour in New Zealand, helped set up two new right to die organizations there, and flew home to Los Angeles. Soon the article appeared in *Women's Own* in a huge center spread, containing as a footnote a request to anybody who knew Mrs. Bettine Elizabeth Eden (née Duggan) to contact me at the *Los Angeles Times*.

Total silence. I was puzzled. I was back in Australia for a death with dignity conference in Melbourne in 1982, another book tour five years later, and then again in 1992 in an extensive nationwide publicity book tour with the controversial *Final Exit*. Every time I pushed my inquiries. Still silence.

When I was promoting the book in Japan, at the press club I met up with the veteran foreign correspondent Murray Sayle, whom I had known when we were both at the *London Sunday Times*. Over lunch I mentioned this strange business of my mother's behavior. To my pleasant surprise, Murray offered to find her if I paid his expenses. Murray is a world-class investigative reporter and a native of Australia, so I knew that if anybody could crack the puzzle, it was him. The only clue I could give him was that Mother had once lived in a house in Lismore, New South Wales, but that was back in 1953 when she had put that address on her first letter to me. Soon he visited Lismore but neither the current householder nor any neighbor had heard of a Mrs. Eden. But the persistent Murray studied the local electoral rolls for hours and eventually found "John Eden (farmer) and Bettine Elizabeth Eden (domestic duties)." Now we had confirmed names to work with. Murray called every person called Eden in New South Wales, to no avail.

Murray studied the voter rolls and telephone books all over Australia and found that there were Edens in West Australia. One in particular was interesting: at 26 Oakover Street, West Freemantle, there was a "Sean Eden" on the electoral roll. That was the name of my half brother. But the address did not have a telephone. A helpful young woman at the council office said that the rates (property taxes) on this address were paid by the public trustee. That was the clue. Murray called him, and he said that Mother had died on October 7, 1991. We were one year late. Because she left no will, the public trustee was trying to find Mother's children in order to wind up the estate. He did not even know that her first married name was Humphry, nor where children were, or their names. He had advertised in British newspapers for us, with no response. Messages were left for Sean to call Murray, and a few days later he did. First part of the mission accomplished. Sean wrote to me; I wrote back. It was clear we were half brothers.

I secured a copy of Mother's death certificate, which immediately solved the mystery of why Mother had never responded during all my very public visits to Australia between 1978 and

1992. She could not. The death certificate gives the cause of death as "multi-organ failure (3 weeks), senile dementia (15 years), cerebrovascular accident (15 years)." A stroke in 1976 had destroyed her mind, resulting in the last fifteen years being spent in a nursing home.

There was a curious coincidence about the date: October 7, 1991. On that same weekend when Mother died in Australia, Ann committed suicide in Oregon, and Aunt Gwen died of old age in Britain.

My *Final Exit* book promotion tour of Australia included Perth, and when the interviews ended, I took the opportunity to drive on to Freemantle to meet my half brother for the first time since 1954. Sean and I had a good visit; he showed me around and took me to an alligator farm. We visited Mother's old house. It was a bleak, tin-roofed house in terrible condition and mostly empty of furniture. Disappointingly, there was no trace of Mother's possessions after fifteen years' absence, nothing left by which I could relate to the final decades of her life. But the area in which the house stood, with its large garden, had become an upscale housing tract. In fact, Mother's decrepit house was now a blight on the district, but the land extremely valuable. Until I appeared on the scene, it could not be sold by the public trustee without first tracing all children. Because of my search, soon Mother's estate was wound up.

Although the silence of the last fifteen years was now explained, it did not clear up the mystery of why Mother chose not to tell me where she lived, nor make any sort of contact. The letters she wrote to me in 1953–54 (which I still have) show a longing to be close to Garth and me. For instance, one letter states, "It's the only goal I've had, hoping to see you boys again." Another example: "I've become very despondent and run down with the worry of not knowing about you. Now I'm a much happier person and looking forward to the time of coming home and seeing my sons, daughters-in-law, and grandchildren." All thirteen letters are signed "Your Loving Mother."

What was even stranger was to learn from Sean that they had returned to Britain twice more, completely unknown to me. They had lived in Southampton when he tried becoming a police cadet, and on another visit had bought a house in Camden Town, London, which was within a couple of miles of my office at the *Sunday Times* and my home in Hackney. We could have bumped into each other! They always went back to Australia after a few months. I asked Sean why Mother went back and forth to Britain—at least five times—always on cargo ships, which took around six weeks each way. This constant long-distance traveling made for a huge gap in his education. So far as I can recollect Sean's answer, he said: "There was something strange about her in this respect. I think she had Alzheimer's." Perhaps it was early-stage Alzheimer's, which can begin from forty years old.

Murray Sayle, who was born in Australia and went to Europe for an extended spell in top-class journalism, offers this opinion of Mother's peripatetic behavior: "It looks to me as if your mother, finding herself as she saw it, was faced with an agonizing choice between Britain and Australia, which meant a choice in effect between you and your brother, young men, and Sean, then hardly more than a baby, came to eliminate the UK and all its inhabitants from her memory—perhaps a question of who, as she saw it at that stage, needed her more. Rough on you, as you must have felt twice-abandoned, but I can only say I sympathize with all those involved, and, again, hope I have helped to ease some pain rather than the reverse."

REDEMPTION

As he got into middle and old age, my father matured and settled down to life in seaside Poole, Dorset, with his third wife, Doris. He kept out of trouble, made a modest living as the organizer of exhibitions, and unexpectedly devoted his life to sailing. The area where he now lived was high income, and the local yacht clubs were socially exclusive and expensive to join. So in 1956, Father and a few friends got permission to put a hut on a promontory of the Blue Lagoon in Poole and appropriately called their outfit the Lilliput Sailing Club. Like Topsy, it grew and grew until a few years later it possessed an elegant clubhouse and berthing facilities. Anybody could join, with any class of boat. Such was the quality of its sailboat-racing program that it was once host and manager of the Olympic Trials.

Roy Humphry was the first commodore of the Lilliput and remained so until 1974. Such was his devotion to the club that he would chair the management meetings and also scrub out the showers if no one else had done it. The club was his life. With Doris, he often sailed his own beautiful teak yacht across the English Channel to France, enjoyed a sumptuous French meal, berthed overnight, and sailed back the next day. Both Garth and I put the checkered past behind us to become firm friends with Father.

One incident very movingly told me that Father had redeemed his young man's reputation as a London playboy and petty fraudster. I needed a trailer for my little sailing dinghy, and Father pointed out a man in the club who had one for sale. I wrote out a check to the man for sixty pounds, the amount he was asking, and handed it to the seller. He looked at my signature and asked: "Are you Roy Humphry's son?" I told him yes. I was fearful. To my astonishment, he handed the check back to me.

"Your father has done so much for me over the years that I couldn't accept full price for this trailer," he said. "Make it twenty pounds."

I wrote out a new check. When handing it over, I averted my head to hide my tears—tears of gladness that I could be proud of my father at last.

He died of a stroke at age seventy-nine, poor as a church mouse but content. Despite the rough ride he had given us as children, all was forgiven. Garth and I willingly paid for his funeral. His memorial service was packed, with standing room only. The Dorset newspapers in their long obituaries spoke glowingly of his sterling work and leadership in local sailing affairs.

Chapter 16

DIVORCE WARS

D URING 1989, ANN'S EMOTIONAL state became progressively worse. Tempers increased and moods blackened. She threatened to cut off all sexual relations between us unless we went into joint marriage counseling. This threat was unnecessary because I went willingly, hoping desperately for an answer to our unhappiness from these expert therapists. My dilemma was that there was fundamentally nothing wrong between us except for her unbalanced, erratic emotional outbursts, plus my inability to understand and cope with them. As yet, I did not know that this condition was defined as a Borderline Personality Disorder, which could be looked up in the classic textbook *DMSR* (*Diagnostic and Statistical Manual of Mental Disorders*).

Ann was beating me over the head—so to speak—continuously with two complaints:

1. My three sons were abominable, ungrateful, and should be completely disregarded. That they lived

    their own lives as grown men six thousand miles away
    made no difference to her hostility.

2. I had "not supported her" during and after the deaths
    of her parents. What she meant was that I did not
    talk with her, over and over, about the details and the
    emotions of the event. It was discussed at intervals,
    but I am not the sort of person who wants to agonize
    for something that happened in the past, over and
    over again. Anyway, she was in therapy twice a week,
    presumably struggling with her problems through
    these professional help outlets.

Suddenly a new and awful crisis hit us, creating a third albatross around my neck. Ann developed breast cancer and so became my second wife to have this diagnosis. Thankfully, unlike Jean, Ann detected the lump early. A test found that it was cancerous, and a successful lumpectomy was quickly performed. The deformity to her breast was fairly insignificant. The heartening difference between Jean's and Ann's breast cancer was that when the lymph nodes were tested in a laboratory, Jean's were riddled with cancer, whereas Ann's were clear. From the start, Jean's death was only a matter of time; Ann's doctor told her that a recurrence was highly unlikely. Additionally, ways of treating cancer were considerably more sophisticated than when Jean was ill sixteen years earlier.

    But although Ann insisted from the start, and continued to say for the rest of her life, that she suffered from what she liked to call "invasive cancer," Jean had fought with every medical procedure and a cool courage to live for as long as she could. What was the most distressing part of this period to me was that Ann kept taunting me: "You cried for Jean, why aren't you crying for me?" My answer was that I—and her doctors—thought she had every chance of living for years (which proved to be the case).

There was no point in my crying. I named other women whom we knew that had also had breast cancer, followed by surgery, and were still living for years—as many as twenty—after the discovery. It made no impression.

Another strange facet of Ann's personality emerged during this cancer crisis. She announced that if the medical tests showed that the cancer was eliminated, she would do something very special in her life. She would not tell me what this was. I assumed that it might be working for Doctors Without Borders or raising cancer prevention funds. Something noble as a gesture of gratitude. After all, she had worked in the Peace Corps in Africa in her twenties. Imagine my astonishment as we got the "all clear" news when Ann announced that the special something was learning to fly an airplane! Which she did, taking lessons in a single-engine aircraft at Eugene Airport.

The comparisons with Jean's terminal illness continued from Ann. Along with her other tantrums—foot-stamping temper flare-ups, and harping on the ingratitude of my sons—it was wearing me down. It was my inability to talk and wrestle with these subjects for hours at a time that was my flaw in my relationship with Ann. I failed her in this respect. We saw a "couple" couple, a man-and-wife therapist team, one Wednesday evening at Ann's request. All I recall of it was that one counselor said: "There is a great gulf between you."

Once back at home I told Ann again that I wanted either a separation or a divorce, at which she turned hysterical for several hours. But then sat down and admitted: "I shouldn't use emotional blackmail." The tension between us was so great that I stalled, saying that I would give the breakup further consideration. It brought temporary peace at around 3 a.m.

This type of emotionally fraught situation is common among couples who are breaking up. So why am I relating this unhappy but normal behavior? Because when I told Ann three days later that I definitely wanted a divorce, a public war broke out. (By chance, Donald Trump was also going through a hugely publicized divorce at the same time, thus we played second fiddle to him.) Ann owned the hobby farm in Monroe, Oregon, where we lived. I had no wish to inconvenience her, and so I went to live in a motel. Pushing a cart around a local supermarket, when publicity about our breakup was massive, I collided with Ann's therapist. "I seem to have left the marriage at a bad time," I remarked spontaneously.

He replied, "There's never a good time to leave a marriage." Perhaps I should have waited longer but I was at a breaking point, mainly through the constant, agonizing comparisons that Ann made between what she considered was her forthcoming death and how Jean and I had had handled hers.

Ann beat me to the divorce court by filing within forty-one days. I was in the course of filing but saw no need to rush my attorney. In three months, hostilities, as they say in war, broke out. Ann went to my old paper, the *Los Angeles Times*, and told them I had abandoned her even as she was recovering from cancer. They chose to ignore the story. Then Ann got a friend to approach the *New York Times* with the same complaint, but spicing it up this time with a claim that I had stolen forty thousand dollars from Hemlock's bank account. On February 8, 1990, the *Times* devoted a half page to our pending divorce and the alleged financial theft, printing all of Ann's claims about my "appalling behavior" that she said showed that I was not the caring person who ran Hemlock but a heartless monster. It was such a lengthy article that a lot of people only got halfway through it before they had had enough. The second half contained my response, in which I stated that Ann was mentally ill and that I left her when I could bear the strain no longer. The *Times* did not have the good ethics of journalism to ask me whether I had stolen the forty thousand dollars, thereby avoiding having to print my denial. Neither did it question why Ann, who was the society's treasurer, had not informed the directors of my alleged theft. Immediately the directors of Hemlock instituted an audit of the society's accounts but found nothing missing. The Internal Revenue Service conducted an audit of Hemlock and also—in the following two years—of me personally. No fraud was found. As is IRS practice, the complainant is also always audited. They found Ann owed six hundred dollars in back taxes on her farm through an accounting error.

Ann began appearing on television—including *Larry King Live* and *The Sally Jesse Raphael Show*—and numerous radio shows, beating the drums of hate against me. When the personal attacks wore thin, she turned her settling of scores on to Hemlock, becoming its Judas. She appeared on radio shows with right to life zealot Rita Marker, denouncing me as a fraud and Hemlock as a sham. I was astonished that an intelligent, educated person could so quickly become such a turncoat on an ethical cause that she had—apparently—embraced publicly for nearly twenty years. Ann approached my long-time Hollywood publicist, Irwin Zucker, wanting to pay him to get her on radio and television shows. He declined, saying that I was his client and that she should find someone else.

Although the divorce was by mutual consent on the grounds of incompatibility, we ended up in the divorce court in Eugene for two days when Ann would not agree to financial terms. She did not emerge well from the hearing when it was revealed that she had gone to the manager of the local Wells Fargo Bank and borrowed ten thousand dollars on the grounds that I had left her penniless. She related to everybody she met that she had been forced into this loan by my abandonment. Under cross-examination it was proven, and she admitted, that at the same time as she was taking out this "hardship loan" she had more than sixty thousand dollars on cash deposit with her investment bank. Anyway, the terms of the breakup were settled by the court: I was instructed to pay alimony, and Ann was ordered to return all my books, private papers, and documents. When, six months later, she had not done this, I had no choice but to take her to court to enforce the divorce court order.

To bolster her self-image, Ann frequently lied. She told people—and once had it printed—that she possessed a PhD from the Shakespeare Institute, a division of the University of Birmingham, in England. True, she had studied there toward a doctorate but never submitted a thesis. She also announced that she had written two novels, neglecting to say that they had never found publishers.

In this second court hearing, Ann told the judge under oath that there were no books or papers. They had been accidentally left outside the farmhouse, then taken away by the trash collector. The judge turned to me and said: "Then what can you do if they're gone?" I admitted defeat. But that was not the end of the story. A few weeks after Ann's suicide a year later, the executor of her estate called me at my office. "Please come round to my office, and bring a truck," he said. When I reached there, he handed over all my library and papers that had supposedly been trashed.

Another documented instance of Ann's untruthfulness was in her will, in which she left her entire estate of some three hundred thousand dollars to her cousin Nancy. But the will contained a sinister lie: Ann told her attorney that she had no children. In fact, she had had a child while living in Toronto in the 1960s and had put him up for adoption because the father would not marry her. Moreover, during the same year as the will was drawn up, the adopted son contacted Ann through the registry that the Canadian government keeps to permit, by mutual consent, adult adoptees to find their biological parents. In her last year of life, he visited her on her farm. She impressed him by flying up to Seattle in her training aircraft to pick him up on his journey from Montreal. When I heard of the reunion, I was delighted for Ann; I had always backed her in her search for the son she called Ian, now named Bill Stone. As much as she enjoyed his visit—so I was told—she could not include him in her will via a codicil because that would reveal her untruth in the original document. Thus, the unfortunate young man was twice abandoned by Ann—as a baby twenty-two years earlier and again a few months after the recent reunion—and never mentioned in her will. He could have challenged the will but he did not know of his omission.

A year after our breakup, Ann filed a lawsuit against me for $6 million in damages for libel, slander, outrageous conduct, negligent infliction of emotional distress, and breach of fiduciary duty. The suit claimed I was coaxing her to commit suicide and wanted to impede her recovery from cancer. It was the first libel suit in my life—and from my ex-wife! These fantastic allegations all hit the newspapers and television in a big way; there was nothing I could do about them because they were protected language within a lawsuit. I was astounded and denied them as being without merit, citing "hell hath no fury like a woman scorned." I then proceeded to mount a defense. First of all, my attorney, Lee Kersten, pointed out that the $6 million damages were unattainable because Ann's attorney had failed to notice that the Oregon legislature had recently capped such damages at $1 million. On top of that, the suit's particulars of my "offenses" were modified downward three times as Ann's attorneys found continued weaknesses in her claims.

The divorce and its aftermath were so bitter that few people could remember such a nasty divorce. A friend who is a forensic psychologist, and had witnessed similar ugly cases, warned me: "Ann will either kill you or kill herself."

As I knew well from a lifetime in journalism, there comes a stage called "discovery," when each side in a lawsuit must reveal to each other all the documents involved in the case. Many litigants are broadsided by this revelation—even Enoch Powell, the racist, was stumped by this rule in his failed libel suit against the *Sunday Times*. I looked in my tax returns for the past fifteen years and saw that I had been taking tax deductions for the continuous fees I had paid to Ann's psychotherapists and psychologists. I provided my attorney with a list, which he sent to Ann's attorneys asking that they provide our side with full medical reports from these experts. I think it surprised them. Additionally, the case was nearing a stage when both sets of lawyers had to take depositions from the witnesses. This is a laborious and expensive procedure, often the biggest cost in a lawsuit, as the evidence is meticulously taken down and later transcribed. Now Ann's lawyers not only had reached that costly stage but had these additional medical witnesses in Canada, England, and California to interview as well.

Within a week, they went into court and asked the judge to allow them to quit the case on the grounds that they could not agree with their client on how the case should be handled. There was time, they said, for Ann to find other lawyers to finish the case. The judge had no alternative but to agree to their choice to dismiss themselves. It initiated the events leading to Ann's death within a few days. When she was told of the law firm's decision to pull out, Ann immediately set in motion a plan to commit suicide and blame me. She had depended on destroying both me and the Hemlock Society with this crushing $1 million law-suit that its failure must have been a bitter blow. It is clear now that not only did she intend suicide but also strove to renew her charge that I murdered Jean. It was her alternative to the failed lawsuit. Ann made a bitter video and arranged with friends for it to be distributed widely to the news media. She composed a suicide note (undated) to me, which read as follows:

> Derek:
> There. You got what you wanted. Ever since I was diagnosed as having cancer, you have done everything conceivable to precipitate my death.
> I was not alone in recognizing what you were doing. What you did—desertion and abandonment and subse-quent harassment of a dying woman—is so unspeakable there are no words to describe the horror of it.
> Yet you know. And others know too. You will have to live with this untiol (sic) you die.
> > May you never, ever forget. Ann

Ann certainly had a powerful way with words, even if they were not always the truth. She was never dying. There is no evidence that her cancer had returned. I certainly had no wish to harass her; it seemed to be the other way around, as she paraded her woes on television and radio and gave interviews to scandal-hungry news-paper reporters. However, Ann knew how enthusiastically the media would revel in this latest piece of the showdown, to which she had been building up for a year. (In a book that is a collec-tion of suicide notes published in 1997, Ann's note was included in the chapter titled "Hate." Author Marc Etkind wrote: ". . . Ann's hate-filled note . . . makes one question her motives. Is

she expressing serious doubts about euthanasia, or is she simply
seeking revenge on her husband?" (. . . *Or Not to Be: A Collection
of Suicide Notes* [Riverhead Books, 1997.])

The true intent of Ann's note—to try to make me feel guilty
for the rest of my life—lay in its total condemnation of me alone.
No mention of her parents, whom she had spent most of her
life excoriating, and no taking a whit of responsibility for her
own life. It was planned as pure character assassination of me,
provoked by the crushing failure to ruin Hemlock and me in the
courts.

Shortly after writing the note (the timeline is not clear),
Ann put one of her horses in a horsebox and drove off in her
pickup truck into the Three Sisters Wilderness Area in the
Cascade Mountains. There she parked at the Three Creeks
Lake, saddled up, and rode about three miles to a secluded
spot. After removing the horse's bridle and saddle and turning him free, she sat down against a tree to watch the sun set
in the western sky. She swallowed a large number of leftover
Vesperax, which she had hoarded since her parents' deaths
five years earlier, washing them down with Chivas Regal, her
favorite whisky. Presumably she died quickly and peacefully
from that lethal combination.

Two things had alerted the local law enforcement officers.
The horse was spotted after it wandered back to its box near the
lake, and friends found the suicide note. A search for Ann by
sheriffs on foot, by horseback, and in helicopter and fixed-wing
aircraft began, lasting six days, which was extensively reported
in the newspapers and on television. The sheriff of Deschutes
County told the media that more than three hundred man-hours
had been spent searching for Ann.

When the Hemlock staff alerted me, as I was preparing to
appear on a television talk show in San Diego, I handed the TV

show over to Faye Girsh and flew back to Eugene to handle the crisis. (The media treated the hunt as though it was for my wife, whereas we had been divorced for two years and I had remarried.) A deputy sheriff found Ann's body, which fortunately had not been attacked by the black bears, coyotes, and foxes that inhabit the local wilderness. Then followed perhaps the saddest television clip I had seen in my life when the local television evening news showed Ann's body, slung over a packhorse, coming down the mountainside. It was like something out of a Western movie. Ann was quietly cremated; her friends and son cast the ashes in a field near the duck pond at her home, Windfall Farm.

I assumed that this awful chapter in my life was drawing to an end with Ann's tragic death. That she committed suicide was not a total surprise because she had attempted it during her first marriage (so her ex-husband told me), at the end of that marriage (so she told me), and came close to doing so earlier that year, in 1991, but was rushed into the psychiatric ward of Eugene's Sacred Heart Hospital. During her time there she was diagnosed, by a psychologist assigned to assess her risk to herself, as having "a mixed kind of disturbance, borderline, mixed with hysterical features." (He offered me this clinical finding when I chanced to meet him the following year.)

But the war was not over. A friend joked to my circle of friends and acquaintances: "Ann's throwing grenades at him from the grave." First there was that vitriolic video and the suicide note circulating freely. I chose not to look at the video—it was obviously a regurgitation of all the old complaints about me. The second was a surprise. As I got off a flight arriving at Eugene Airport, I was met at the terminal entrance by about thirty journalists and television crewmen. "What's up?" I asked.

The journalists explained that a copy of Ann's suicide note had been forwarded to my biggest right to die opponent, Rita

Marker, who promptly made it public. This version of her suicide note had an added footnote referring to my first wife:

> Rita: My final words to Derek. I know Jean actually died
> of suffocation. I could never say it until now; who would
> believe me? Do the best you can. Ann

The final five words of this footnote indicated that Ann wanted
this to be her final damaging publicity stunt. Mrs. Marker made
sure it was.

So, did I murder Jean? the pack of journalists asked. I told
them that I had assisted in the suicide of Jean, by her choice
and request. Ann was completely unknown to any of us at the
time; in fact, I think she was in Canada. How could Ann claim
to know that I had suffocated Jean? Where was her evidence? I
had admitted in the memoir *Jean's Way* that had the drugs not
worked, I would have been obliged to suffocate her. But that had
not been necessary. I pointed out to the media that the British
police had done a six-month investigation into the case, interviewing all friends, family, and doctors, and found that I had not
committed any crime. By law, the whole case had to be reviewed
by the UK's director of public prosecutions. He cleared me in
a letter to my attorney in London, adding a comment on how
brave he thought Jean had been. The media recorded all this
scandal, and it made the usual headlines. *Vanity Fair* magazine
did a lengthy hatchet job on me, as did ABC's television show
Prime Time. The *New York Times* color magazine printed an
extensive blow-by-blow account, extensively syndicated at home
and abroad, which was fairly balanced. Ann's son wrote a bitter
letter to *Vanity Fair* condemning me without hearing the other
side of the story. Nine years later I received a surprising phone
call from him in which he immediately said: "I forgive you for

what happened to my mother. I have no more anger." I was about to say that there was nothing for which I wanted forgiveness but instead asked him if he had by now met his real father, Arthur Brunner. He said he had—and that seemed to be the reason for his now tolerant attitude.

A woman whom I did not know approached me with a frightening story concerning Ann when she was in the psychiatric ward the same year as her suicide. This person said that she, too, was an inpatient at the time. A man was brought into care who had burned down his wife's house. She overheard Ann asking him if he would also burn down my house, to which he agreed. My informant had recently spotted this arsonist in a supermarket and feared he would harm me. We kept the front gates and doors carefully locked for months to come. Nothing happened.

And the "grenades" kept coming. A few months after Ann's death, a display advertisement appeared in the *Los Angeles Times* offering the private papers and journals of the late Ann Wickett Humphry for sale. It described her as a writer and cofounder of the Hemlock Society. Persons interested had to apply to an attorney in Eugene to be able to view and bid for the collection. Surprised, I made inquiries and found that Ann had neglected to burn her journals and papers—even though she lived on twenty acres where small bonfires were not infrequent. She had thrown them into a trash bag, and then while en route with horsebox to her death on the mountain, had tossed the bag into the public garbage dump at Monroe. It seems that as the subsequent hunt for her became headlines and TV news, somebody who had seen her throw away the bag climbed back into the huge dumpster and retrieved it. That scumbag took it to an attorney, who then offered it for sale. Muckraking journalists from all over the US flew to Oregon to view the collection, but none made any offers. The papers must have contained no new scandal. The board of the Hemlock Society eventually decided to offer one thousand dollars for the papers in order to destroy them. That gave us the opportunity to inspect them ourselves. I sent Hemlock's staff attorney, Cheryl Smith, to take a look. She reported back that the journals seemed full of self-pity, a curious disappointment over her animals (which was untypical previously)—and also a shock. For in her journals Ann revealed that she had discussed with close friends paying a hit man to have me assassinated and then blaming the right to life movement for the murder. (Hit men can be found in America—plus Ann was wealthy enough to pay the usual fifty-thousand-dollar fee.) Happily, there is no evidence that she went ahead with the plan, but it was yet another troubling revelation of her dark thoughts. Hemlock's offer to purchase the papers was rejected.

All this tragedy and scandal went on against a background— quite independently—of my being for a while the best-known author in the US. Two months before Ann died, my book *Final Exit* had become the number-one best-selling nonfiction book in the US, the world's largest book market. Both the *New York Times* best-seller lists and *Publishers Weekly* maintained it at the top for several months. Thus I was operating on two levels of fame—one of tragedy and one of achievement. I appeared on almost all the national television talk shows, with the Ann divorce never mentioned. The anchors were interested in why a book on suicide for the terminally ill would take the top slot in American nonfiction literature.

The director of the International Anti-Euthanasia Task Force, Rita Marker, in 1993 published a one-sided book entitled *Deadly Compassion: The Death of Ann Humphry and the Truth About Euthanasia* (William Morrow & Co., 1995). It was 310 pages of bile drawn entirely from Ann, combining truths, half-truths, and untruths that I did not bother to contradict. It contained five pictures of me. It sold poorly. I inquired into its sales from the manager of a chain bookstore in Eugene, where it ought to have sold best, and he replied that he had not sold a single copy, returning them all to the publisher. Unable to stand on its own merit, both the hardback and the paperback editions leaned heavily for their promotion on my best-seller *Final Exit*, pasting its title all over the jackets.

The media's attempt to take me down failed because in the US there is an attitude of tolerance toward people in trouble. And as one Hollywood writer cheerfully told me: "Now you've been in troubles, you are much more interesting." My speaking engagements never ceased, and my books sold worldwide. Membership in Hemlock began to pick up again, perhaps bolstered by all the publicity about the book and the divorce.

Nevertheless, I wish Ann's illness had not caused this painful war and her chosen demise at age forty-nine. It took this self-deliverance to be rid of her demons. When in good health, the handsome Ann was loving, noble, thoughtful, generous, and caring. Nowadays, with the passage of years, I choose to remember more of the good things about her than the opposite.

Chapter 17

FAREWELL TO HEMLOCK

Controversial in death as in life, "Hemlock Society USA" as a name died suddenly on June 13, 2003, in a boardroom in Denver, Colorado. It was twenty-three years old. Public relations experts and political strategists, leaning heavily on focus groups, were on hand to usher in the death knell. Months of agonizing debate had preceded the decision because no one could think of a better name.

Hemlock was by now the largest and oldest right to die organization remaining in the US, fighting for voluntary euthanasia and physician-assisted suicide to be made legal for terminally and hopelessly ill adults. (There had been larger organizations, but they had kept what might be called a "passive euthanasia" agenda, ran out of funding, and were closed down.)

As it twisted and turned at the whims of shuttling board members, Hemlock had many homes: Santa Monica, Los Angeles, Eugene (Oregon), and Denver. Sadly, it never reached its rightful home in the nation's capital, Washington, DC, where it could have had the most influence. Hemlock's principal achievements during a stormy life were as follows:

- Educate and advise thousands of dying people to know how to bring about their peaceful ends when dying, trapped in a ruined body, or just plain terminally old, frail, and tired of life. Hemlock never snooped into why people were joining or buying its "how-to" literature. It was the individual's choice and private affair.
- Give help through specialized literature and moral support. Not until later did the organization provide hands-on assistance to people to die because it needed, in the ethical climate of the 1980s, to stay within the law, although many of its members quietly, unofficially, did see one another off.
- Draft and launch the first model law governing euthanasia and assisted suicide in America in 1986, from which many others to follow were adapted and refined. This law was introduced by Senior Senator Frank Roberts into the Oregon legislature in 1991 as Senate Bill 1141. Vehemently and prominently opposed by Oregon's clergy, it did not get beyond the first committee hearing. Nevertheless, it made its mark as the first legislation of its type to come before lawmakers in the US. Why would Senator Roberts introduce such a law? He believed in voluntary euthanasia and died soon after of cancer. Hemlock's failed law was to be the pacesetter to the successful Oregon Death With Dignity Act passed in 1994 by the voters, thereby evading the nervous, deadly hand of the state legislature.

- Financially and physically back referenda in California, Washington State, Michigan, Oregon, and Maine. Though all lost, most got nearly 50 percent of the vote. Only Oregon succeeded (in 1994 and again when challenged in 1997). That law has survived the Bush Administration's threat of extinction via the courts, right up to the US Supreme Court.

- Launch a national "Caring Friends" program in 1999 so that maximum personal support and assistance in dying—within the law—could be ensured to every member. No member need die alone or in agony. This was a free program. Credit for starting this kindly program goes to Faye Girsh, Lois Schaffer, the late Sallie Troy, and Richard MacDonald. (Nowadays, after Hemlock was closed, it has a more business-like name: "Client Services.")

Strangely, Hemlock's cause of death was its very name and success—and because it had a large bank balance and membership list that others coveted. Never before had the organization been so large in staff (twenty-six), with membership rising again, or so financially sound ($3 million) as in 2003. The striking name of the nonprofit organization was its entrée, its cachet, and its PR flag as it fought for twenty-three years against the relentless forces of the religious right. It was the voice of choice in dying through the decade of the 1980s during a time when Ronald Reagan and Jerry Falwell claimed to be the nation's defining moral forces.

Hemlock came to be sourced in medical and legal texts and has become respected as one of the pioneer right to die organizations in the world. In 2000 in Boston, Hemlock hosted the largest international conference held on the right to die.

Few school textbooks are without a proactive essay on this subject. As I've said, I retired from Hemlock in 1992 in order to return to being a writer and communicator. I'm not the CEO-managerial type. But over the next ten years, I spoke for Hemlock at meetings all over America.

In the 1990s, Hemlock declined in membership from forty-six thousand to eighteen thousand as other groups, started after state initiative campaigns, also took up the cudgels. Anyway, my maverick little book entitled *Final Exit* showed everybody with seventeen dollars to spare exactly how to exercise his or her ultimate civil liberty. Ownership of the book carried no obligation to be a member of anything. Inadvertently, the book had pulled the rug out from under Hemlock's membership base because the majority of enrollers had joined only to get information for their own deliverance at some point. Only a relative few joined Hemlock to fight for law reform. Now the fundamental information was a paperback in bookstores. But in 2002, before the name change, membership in Hemlock had gone back up to thirty-three thousand.

A great many people tell me that *Final Exit* was beset with numerous lawsuits. This canard has spread over the years. In fact, there was only one lawsuit brought against the book. The week after the *New York Times* reported that the book had earned Hemlock $2 million, predictably, a lawsuit followed. (This figure was what Hemlock earned gross; printing and other fees swallowed $750,000.) The folly of this lawsuit was that it was from the family of a man who had killed himself by piping the exhaust fumes of his pickup into the cab. My book expressly says that this is a lousy way to end your life—it may not work and is a danger to others. Anyway, Hemlock's lawyers answered that, under the First Amendment to the US Constitution, a book cannot be sued. The case was dropped without any court hearings.

A Tree, a Weed, or an Exit

The noun "hemlock" can refer to a conifer tree or a waterweed. It was the root of the weed that was used in classical Greek and Roman times as a deadly poison when death by suicide was either ordered by the state or chosen by a rational person. Today we have lost the knowledge of how to effectively use hemlock as a lethal potion, and probably the ancients glossed over just how painful it was to die that way. For over two thousand years, Socrates personified the drinking of hemlock as a symbol of rational suicide.

And it is today's politicians and their strategists, plus a few focus groups, that have condemned the name as "tied to that fellow and poisoner Socrates." The name, some said, would hinder passage of legislation. The membership appeared divided about the name change; none could suggest a good, prim alternative, although some four hundred monikers were considered. Wags suggested the Not-Quite-Dead-Yet Society, the Socrates Society, and the Final Exit Society.

However, Socrates' death in 399 BC was a noble and self-chosen one, and he spent hours discussing with his colleagues whether he should accept either the death sentence inflicted by the courts for corrupting the youth of Athens or go to a lonely exile on a barren island. Essentially, that is what the Hemlock Society was about: not hasty and hurtful suicide, but thoughtful and rational reasons for an accelerated death.

William Batt, a former director of the group, wrote in his essay "Why Hemlock as a Name and Symbol": "The choice of the hemlock root as a symbol of our movement is quite apt for more than one reason. The first because it symbolizes the principle of personal choice central to Socrates' action. The second because Socrates faced choices [exile] unacceptable to him much like terminally ill people today. The third because it focuses centrally on the place of self in society in a way that was vital to Socrates in his time as well as for people living today."

It appears that contemporary people who know little or nothing about Socrates or other ancient Greeks who supported rational suicide won the day. Some had never liked the name; others saw it as black or gallows humor. And some worried about its connotations of poison and suicide. True, some timid persons were worried about what the neighbors would think if it was common knowledge that they were members of the Hemlock Society. Thinking people who had studied Plato and were passably well-read regarded Hemlock as a name with special philosophical meaning. Just hearing the name spoken instantly informed many people exactly what its purpose was. But some felt it was too elitist a name.

Surveys showed that a great many people associated the Hemlock Society with Dr. Jack Kevorkian, although there was never any affiliation with him and not much empathy. But Hemlock benefited financially from his notoriety because both he and Hemlock were big news in the 1990s. The change of "brand name" was a blow to the new organization; it had two years of devastating losses in 2004 and 2005, when income dropped by half a million. The newly merged group was doing huge direct mailings with its fresh name, causing the return rate to drop from 1 percent when it was Hemlock to 0.25 percent when it became End-of-Life Choices and then Compassion and Choices.

Putting the case for name change in the newsletter, staffer Jane Sanders wrote: "We [also] need access to the halls of government in the states and in Washington, DC, access that the name Hemlock is currently denying us. The name Hemlock has a history of earnest defiance but much of it is also baggage,

baggage that we can no longer afford to have weighing us down or interfering with our being able to partner with such important and powerful organizations as AARP ("A Rose is a Rose: Hemlock by Any Other Name," *End-of-Life Choices* magazine, Vol. 2, No. 2, Spring 2003). What exactly was in the baggage Ms. Sanders discreetly did not reveal to her readers.

IDENTITY LOSS

When the board switched its name from Hemlock Society USA to End-of-Life Choices, the new group jettisoned its famous logo—a wisp of the graceful hemlock weed bending in the breeze—and also the motto "Good Life, Good Death," which I had adopted. Madison Avenue types rushed in to dress up a fresh, politically correct image. Yet change of designation risked a huge loss of name recognition and loyalty built up over twenty years by hundreds of volunteers nationwide. In 2005, the group merged with Compassion in Dying, based in Portland, Oregon, which had been losing money steadily, was not nearly as much a grassroots organization as Hemlock, and was one-third its size.

Additionally, the disappearance of Hemlock could mean that many of the public would tend to think that it had gone out of operation or assume it had changed its mission. Given Hemlock's healthy bank balance and large membership, it seemed to me as though a mouse was swallowing a cat!

But Hemlock's leadership was divided on the value of a name change and merger with a smaller group that was taking command. Consequently, in 2004 those who were dissatisfied with the mergers and transfers (none of which was approved by memberships—they were board decisions) broke away and formed the Final Exit Network. The all-volunteer Network confined itself to guidance for people who were dying or hopelessly ill and vowed to keep clear of politics and courts. Its purpose was to continue the model of the Caring Friends program, providing direct and personal information and support to members with incurable illnesses, whose suffering prompted them to consider ending their lives.

By 2008, the US right to die movement nationally had narrowed down to four organizations: Compassion and Choices, Death With Dignity National Center, the Final Exit Network, and my group, the Euthanasia Research and Guidance Organization (ERGO). Those groups operating out of New York such as Concern for Dying and the Society for the Right to Die, which had been powerful in the 1970s and 1980s, went out of existence altogether because they had concentrated on passive euthanasia via living wills and similar documents. Critical of me and others who also sought voluntary euthanasia and assisted suicide, they lost touch with the public need for something more positive. In 2007, three small groups that had been chapters first of Hemlock and then of Compassion and Choices broke away, became independent, and reverted to the original name Hemlock (of San Diego, Florida, and Illinois). They claimed that without the name Hemlock they could not attract sufficient members or money. Compassion and Choices claimed it still owned the Hemlock name and began legal proceedings against the Hemlock Society of San Diego to force it to alter its name.

Naturally, I was disappointed to see Hemlock disappear as a national organization, and its successors seem rather lifeless by comparison with the sizzling voter initiative campaigns of the 1980s and 1990s. Research and records, which I had built up for twenty-five years, were considered unnecessary, so the Hemlock Library was dismantled and given away. Hemlock's great success inevitably earned it rivals and enemies who were jealous of its fame and coveted its money and mailing list. Right to die supporters were confused about who was doing what. The whole American right to die movement took a huge hit, from which it is still trying to recover.

Chapter 18

KEVORKIAN AND ME

T HE RELEASE OF DR. Jack Kevorkian from prison in June 2007 was welcome news. He suffered the eight years of imprisonment with calm and fortitude and deserved a peaceful retirement. Three times Dr. Kevorkian had been acquitted of assisting suicides when the patient had switched on his "Mercitron" machine themselves in order to allow poisonous substances to enter their bodies via tubes that the doctor had inserted. Whether this method of assisted suicide was lawful was a moot point—juries would not convict when they heard the evidence of suffering and death by request. Moving to euthanasia in the case of Thomas Youk was Kevorkian's undoing. Youk had advanced ALS and badly wanted to die, and his family supported him in this. Filming himself in action, Kevorkian injected lethal substances into the veins in Youk's wrist. Regardless of the humanity of the action, in Anglo-American law books, this is murder via the long-standing principle that you cannot ask to be killed. This probably comes from St. Augustine's pronouncement in the fourth century that only God gives life, and only He takes it away.

Law enforcement authorities in Michigan were tired of Kevorkian and his noisy acquittals, so they did nothing despite Youk's death certificate saying that the cause of death was "homicide." Kevorkian wanted to make a cause célèbre out of his incursion into euthanasia, so he went to Mike Wallace at *60 Minutes* and filmed a segment in which he dared the district attorney to charge him with murder or Kevorkian had won the test case. Within a week Kevorkian was charged with both assisted suicide and murder. This time he dispensed with the services of the clever lawyer Geoffrey Fieger, who had got him off on previous occasions. It is an old legal saying that he who defends himself in court has a fool for a client. The prosecution outsmarted Kevorkian in a situation where an observant defense counsel may have spotted the ploy: at the last minute they dropped the assisted suicide charge and proceeded only with the murder charge. The difference is that in assisted suicide cases the defense can call evidence of suffering and choice, whereas in murder cases this cannot be done. Only evidence of the action and who did it can be admitted as evidence.

Kevorkian had planned to call Youk's widow and brother to establish how much suffering was involved and how strongly they agreed to Kevorkian's humanitarian actions. The judge ruled this inadmissible evidence, leaving Kevorkian to make the case himself. The jury had the plain evidence of the video in front of them, along with the judge's strictures that they had only to decide whether or not Kevorkian injected Youk with poison. The jury found him guilty of second-degree murder, and he received a sentence of ten to twenty-five years. Then Kevorkian banked on appeals to higher courts for acquittal and to create a legal precedent. Here he was mistaken: the case was straightforward murder in the eyes of the law, with no ambiguities or legal slip-ups on which to base an effective appeal. There were appeals, but they were little more than formalities.

After eight years, Kevorkian was allowed to ask the parole board for release for good behavior. He also promised never to assist any more suicides, to confine himself to working for a change in the law, which he said he had wished he had done in the past. But the idea that he might have any influence on further developments seems fairly unlikely. Kevorkian was never a part of the organized right to die movement and publicly scoffed at its efforts in the 1990s to change the law. He was a lone ranger on this controversial issue.

The general public is split on the worth of his contribution to achieving so-called "death with dignity" for the terminally ill adult. Many in the health professions were and are skeptical about Kevorkian's style of assisted deaths back in the 1990s. Patients flying into Michigan one day and being found dead the next is not their idea of caring, cautious medical practice. Political activists in the right to die movement in the 1990s dreaded the thought that Kevorkian might show up during their law reform campaigns because he was such a negative figure in their opinion polls. As a freelance helper nicknamed "Dr. Death," he personified everything that the lawmakers sought to avoid. They wanted a sensible "doctor prescribing law" that provided rules and guidelines, with a fourteen-day waiting period.

Claims that he launched the right to die movement and was responsible for the introduction of living wills and hospices are wildly inaccurate. The Hemlock Society was already ten years old with twenty thousand members before Kevorkian surfaced publicly in 1990. California passed the first living will law in 1976. Hospices were opening in America in the middle 1970s.

I met Kevorkian only once, in my Hemlock Society office in Los Angeles by appointment, in 1988. Straight out he explained that he intended to set up a clinic for assisted suicides and asked if Hemlock would supply him with clients. Strange as it seemed to him, I was not enthusiastic. For as much as I admire the segment on euthanasia in the 1973 movie *Soylent Green*—with Edward G. Robinson getting assisted death from beautiful nurses and handsome, white-coated doctors, with Beethoven's Pastoral Symphony playing in the background of an elegant clinic—it is not what would work in real life. The enemies of euthanasia continually harp on the likelihood of abuse if such a service were legal and widely available, and therefore it followed that jumping into a taxi and racing to a commercial clinic is where misbehavior and mistakes are most likely to happen. The place for voluntary euthanasia is in the home, accompanied by watchful friends and caring family, as chosen by the patient, with the services of a willing doctor who possesses signed releases according to law. In the fairly rare cases of a patient who cannot be moved, euthanasia in hospital is appropriate.

I told Kevorkian of my aversion to clinical euthanasia, adding that Hemlock was currently backing a citizen voter initiative in California to change the law to allow voluntary euthanasia and physician-assisted suicide. "You will get huge publicity for your campaign," he argued.

I told him: "I don't think we can at one and the same time be an acceptable campaigner for law reform on this issue while also blatantly breaking the law." Kevorkian immediately stomped out of my office, muttering something about Hemlock and me being pathetically weak. He has never communicated with me since, although I have written friendly notes to him and contributed to his defense fund in the Wouk case. It did not help our relationship when *Newsweek* asked me for a telephone comment on his first (Janet Adkins) case in 1990. I told the reporter: "It is not death with dignity to die in the back of a van. But as her own doctors had refused help, what other choice did she have?" Unfortunately, and perhaps deliberately, the reporter left out the second sentence—thus it looked as though I had made a harsh criticism of Kevorkian. Many journalists love to practice the "dog eat dog" principle of having like-minded people attack each other.

Later in a press conference, Kevorkian said that in the Adkins case I had chastised him severely. I wrote to Kevorkian to explain about the clipped *Newsweek* quotation but I never heard back. The damage was done.

This is how Jack Lessenbury in *Esquire* magazine of April 1997 reported that 1988 incident:

> "I told him no." (me)
> Kevorkian got up and left. . . . Dr. Death was mad, really. As far as he was concerned, Humphry no longer existed. "Well, he's just another Hemlock 'hypocrite,' Kevorkian recalls thinking as he drove away."

At a National Press Club luncheon in 1996, Kevorkian was several times asked about me. He retorted: "I don't know why you keep going to Derek Humphry. He started the Hemlock Foundation, and he thinks he is the grandfather of this thing. He didn't do anything new. We were aware of euthanasia. When I contacted him and asked him first to send me patients who had come to him for help, he didn't send them" (Press Club minutes, July 29, 1996). Although it is true that I would not (in Los Angeles) direct dying patients to Dr. Kevorkian in a suicide clinic, over the years I gave to hundreds of inquirers his home contact address in Michigan.

Kevorkian's main complaint against me is that I am not a physician. Of course not; I am a communicator. Accomplishing societal changes and achieving sensible law reform require many types of people. Nobody can do it alone. The passage of the Oregon law was a team achievement; I merely started the ball rolling in that state eight years earlier. Kevorkian expected to reform the law alone, and—as a recent biography reveals—he expected a Nobel Prize for doing so. But as this book so obviously shows, we went about the same mission in extremely different ways, both caring and authentic.

There is no further need for Dr. Kevorkian's type of services. (He died in 2011.) More significantly, the right to die movement has changed considerably in the last ten years. There are now two national organizations, Compassion and Choices and the Final Exit Network, that will find ways to help suffering, dying people to a speedy and peaceful—and legal—end, if that is what they want.

Certainly Dr. Kevorkian is to be thanked for helping some 130 people to die who obviously wanted his aid in doing so. But he would not move out of his local county; therefore, those who could not travel to him went on suffering. Also, if he had not challenged law enforcement on television to prosecute him, he could have continued to help people instead of languishing in jail. I would like to see a new provision in the homicide laws that would allow (which it sternly does not now) a defendant to plead that it was a merciful killing, upon request, and introduce evidence to that effect. Then let the jury decide whether such drastic action was justified.

There have been—and are—other retired doctors in America who will travel to different places to help dying people who are in great suffering to escape from their pain-racked bodies. (Don't ask me to name them—they are adverse to publicity in order to continue their medicine of mercy.) Kevorkian assiduously courted publicity as his way to shock his medical profession into seeking a change in the law. The media went crazy over the startling sight of a doctor with a suicide machine killing patients upon request. Unheard of! Therefore, I thank Dr. Kevorkian for the huge public interest he aroused in the 1990s around this issue. He will go down in history as a major catalyst for reform by getting public attention via the media's morbid fascination.

Around the same time, shrewd people in Oregon planned to change the law forbidding assisting death in that state. In 1994, with a citizens' vote, they succeeded in putting the Death With Dignity Act on the statute books and then fought all the way to the US Supreme Court to successfully defend it. Some thirty dying people in Oregon take advantage of this law every year. In the coming years, there will be a more receptive climate for law reform in the area of death and dying in more states. The Oregon model marks the way forward to this ultimate civil liberty— the right to die in a manner of one's own choosing.

New Technology

It became obvious around 2000 that legal reform on assisted suicide—despite Oregon—was a long way off, so John Hofsess in Canada, Philip Nitschke in Australia, and I in Oregon started a shadow group calling itself New Technology in Self-Deliverance, or NuTech for short. It has some twenty members, all experienced in assisting in dying. We do not name the membership, for some are doctors, nurses, and social workers. The group has no officers, no bylaws, and no constitution; it comes together once or twice a year by common agreement. The original aim was to develop a method by which a person could kill themselves without involving doctors or family—a stopgap way of self-deliverance from suffering until laws were reformed on a wider scale.

At first, NuTech looked at how deep-sea diving equipment might be modified so that instead of saving life, it ended it. An underwater rebreathing machine was adapted to be an above-ground debreather. It worked, but was too cumbersome and needed expert assistance to be set up for the patient. With the help of the anesthesiologists on our team, we looked at how people might choose to die by the intake of inert gases—such as helium, argon, and neon. These gases are not generally considered lethal, but what we noticed was that these are killer gases when put in an enclosed space around a person's head, driving out the oxygen without which the brain cannot live. The inert gas caused brain death when breathed. We found that the most effective, and easily obtainable, gas was the helium that is used to blow up party balloons. The balloons you see floating on the end of their strings are inflated by pure helium, which can be bought at toy stores and party stores. I will not name the giant company that distributes helium internationally, for although it is aware that we have been using its product for auto-euthanasia for a few years now, the company seems not to mind provided its name is kept out of the subject. Right to die use is a pinprick compared to its enormous business volume.

Helium, which comes from underground holes in the Midwest and West of the United States, is not flammable, not dangerous when freely moving in the air, and not explosive (otherwise it would not be sold to millions of children worldwide). The NuTech team developed a procedure by which the gas could be piped from the little tank into a plastic bag, which the person wishing to die could pull over their head and then tighten at the neck. The person wishing to die turns on the tap of the tank. Coma comes in a few seconds; death in four to five minutes. The cause of death is brain damage, not suffocation. Some people are instinctively averse to putting a plastic bag over their head, which all by itself can kill in thirty minutes. But the helium inside a plastic bag works so rapidly that the aesthetics or phobias of being inside a plastic bag are so fleeting as to be unimportant.

The value of this method of self-deliverance from suffering is that, although suicide and attempted suicide are no longer crimes anywhere, assistance in suicide often is a felony. Even if a state does not have a specific legal prohibition, it might bring a manslaughter charge. However, the method developed by NuTech insists that the patient turns on the valves of the gas tank, thereby committing suicide. Family and friends may be standing by; that is not a crime. Should the deceased have asked that their way of death not be disclosed, no autopsy can show that an inert gas was used, provided the equipment is thrown in a trash can. I recommend the method be made known to law enforcement authorities so as to forestall any police inquires as to cause of death. But people may have other reasons to handle it differently.

The "helium hood method," as it is known, is widely used in the US. Those doctors who discreetly help terminally ill people who want a hastened death prefer this way. It is quicker and less likely to cause vomiting than lethal drugs taken orally—which can take between thirty minutes and five hours to be effective. I am aware of some two hundred such accelerated deaths in the US; I am sure there are many more I do not know about. The meeting of minds at NuTech has bequeathed the invention to society at no charge. When development was going on, ERGO and Hemlock supplied the money to defray the cost of bringing in experts from around the world. NuTech was never a secret organization; it merely flew under the radar, as they say. The third edition of my book *Final Exit* contains a chapter on this method, along with illustrations, which means that coroners and medical examiners know well what is going on. Openness has always been my strategy. In November 2008 in Paris, NuTech held a workshop on methods of self-deliverance attended by experts from around the world.

THE "PEACEFUL PILL"

For many years an urban myth has persisted that there exists a little red pill that, when swallowed, brings instant death, thus wonderfully relieving the sufferer from further pain. I have had scores of requests for it from folk who genuinely believed such a fatal capsule was freely available. It has been called the "Drion pill" (after a Dutch judge of that name who pushed the idea in the 1990s), the "Last Will Pill," and much more recently and popularly, the "peaceful pill."

But this magic tablet does not exist, unless you include a cyanide capsule that only the secret spy services are able to obtain. (Even then it is a painful—if fast—death that you would not want family to observe.) Compounds derived from puffer fish and some Australian snails are equally lethal—in seconds—but they do not, of course, come in pill form. Over the years, I have discussed the peaceful pill in my books *Final Exit* (pages 110 and 139) and in *The Good Euthanasia Guide* (page 21). Because such a lethal pill does not yet exist, the term has come to mean any form of painless, quick, dignified death that the patient wishes to have. It is a metaphor, not an object.

The most deadly substance on the market is pentobarbital (often called Nembutal commercially), which is a barbiturate and powerful sleep aid. It is the substance used in medical euthanasia in countries where that action is legal. Worldwide, it is always by prescription—a script that few doctors will write because its connection with suicide is notorious. Even with pentobarbital's high toxicity, it is still necessary to swallow nine grams (i.e., 90 pills) of it orally to ensure certain death—hardly pill popping! The term has come back into attention with the publication of Dr. Philip Nitschke's book *The Peaceful Pill Handbook*. Nevertheless, he is careful to point out that the handbook outlines numerous methods of ending one's life, not a single way out.

Thus, the hunt for the deadly elixir or pill continues. Currently, the favored means of exit in the US is the careful inhalation of helium gas. But what we really need is legal, medical, voluntary euthanasia and assisted suicide in all countries so that there is no need for these improvised pills and gases.

(Note: From 2016 onward, some of the helium sold commercially to the public—mainly for toy balloon inflation—is twenty percent diluted, making it ineffective for self-deliverance. Pure helium or nitrogen can be used.)

Chapter 19

WHERE WE ARE NOW

Now in my mid-80s, I have been happily married to Gretchen Crocker since 1990, a year before Ann took her life. Odd as it seems, I first met Gretchen when she was a friend of Ann's. They went horse riding together. Nothing romantic happened between us—in fact, Gretchen thought I was a rather stuffy bore. But after the divorce, Ann's farm manager, Jose Mendoza, called me one evening to say that he had seen Ann hiding a suitcase under the hay in the barn. When he looked in it, he found it was stuffed with financial papers, insurance policies, and bank statements, all of which had my name on them. These papers were essential to the running of my life; when previously my attorney had asked for them, he was informed that they had been accidentally destroyed.

Jose remained loyal to Ann, but his conscience told him that I should know about the contents of this suitcase. As with almost all of her friends, Ann had broken ties with Gretchen, so it occurred to me to telephone her and ask if she would mind going over to the hay barn and retrieving the suitcase, which she did in the dead of night. The next day we met for breakfast, and I was given my personal and financial papers, but not my literary papers and books, which were to be the subject of another strange sequence. To express my gratitude, I asked Gretchen if she would like to see a movie with me. We began dating and gradually became a couple. After all the high-powered women I had known, this farmer's daughter was an oasis of calm and thoughtfulness, which I badly needed for the tumultuous few years to follow.

For the last twenty-six years, Gretchen and I have lived in a two-bedroom wooden house on top of Fern Ridge Hill, near Eugene, Oregon, with—on a clear day—a magnificent view across seventy miles to the Cascade Mountains. We have a mongrel dog named Molly, a black cat named Max, and a lumbering Vietnamese potbelly pig called Isabella. The love and peace that Gretchen has brought to the autumn of my life have been one of the greatest rewards of my life. Her worst criticism of me is that I am a workaholic.

From an outbuilding at my home, I have run the tiny Euthanasia Research and Guidance Organization (ERGO) since 1993. It has no staff, outsourcing any work I cannot do. ERGO is a nonprofit organization with its directors spread across California (Faye Girsh, EdD), Canada (Ruth von Fuchs), and the Netherlands (Aycke Smook, MD, retired). ERGO sells books, distributes pro-euthanasia literature, talks to people who still have questions after reading *Final Exit*, and briefs journalists and students. The organization maintains two websites (www.finalexit.org and www.assistedsuicide.org), a web bookstore, a blog, and a news Listserv/mailing list. ERGO provided most of the money to fund the research of NuTech, which resulted in the helium hood method. Both as a paperback and e-book, *Final Exit* continues to sell vigorously after twenty-five years.

Additionally, I am an advisor to the World Federation of Right to Die Societies (www.worldrtd.net), by virtue of having been its president 1988–1990.

I also chair the advisory board of the Final Exit Network (www.finalexitnetwork.org), which I consider to be the successor to the original Hemlock Society. Started in 2003, it provides—to approved cases of terminal and hopeless illness—a guide who will monitor, but not actually assist, the hastened end of a member of the Network. Like ERGO, it has no office and is entirely staffed by volunteers, with the exception of some outsourcing.

Thirty and More Years

People sometimes ask me how it is that for more than thirty years I have been hammering away at the need to provide dying and hopelessly ill adults with (a) the knowledge to bring their lives to an end, if they choose; and (b) law reform to provide the option of voluntary euthanasia and assisted suicide. Am I an obsessive personality? After all, five books, a video film, dozens of speeches, and several hundred television and radio appearances around the world, as well as talking with countless people about the problems with ending their lives to escape suffering, is perhaps an overload. (I do not talk to persons with mental illness, including depression, preferring to pass them on to qualified experts who will try to help.)

In the 1970s some accused me of writing *Jean's Way* and campaigning publicly for the issue out of guilt over helping Jean to die. Yet I have never felt any guilt for my part in Jean's chosen way of death; rather that it is a duty of love between spouses to respond to such an important request. I would have felt guilt had I not helped her die, allowing her to suffer more than she wanted. As I have since learned, from long experience, some spouses will help and others feel they cannot—and I respect that. As my work broadened—more and different books were published, and reforming legislation was campaigned for—people ceased to make that particular accusation of my having guilty feelings. Did I write the books and form Hemlock and ERGO to make money? That also was an accusation made early in my right to die career with the success of *Jean's Way*. But I have been a professional writer since 1945. All money I have ever earned has been from words; and all writers use all or part of their life experience for their material. Also, my profits from *Jean's Way* funded the first year of the existence of the Hemlock Society until it became self-supporting, and the financial success of *Final Exit* later put that organization's income into the million-dollar bracket for the first time.

Gerry Larue, the first Hemlock president, once explained my perseverance by saying, "Derek is like a dog with a rag; he won't let go of things once he gets going."

But it really springs from my lifelong instinct to want to change things for the better and make the world a better place. I have always been an idealist. As soon as I gained a senior foothold in journalism, I wanted to get away from murders and aircraft crashes, and more to report and write about subjects of social concern, as you have seen from earlier chapters. Jean is responsible for my involvement in the right to die issue by the way she chose to die—little did she think she was anticipating a social trend that today's lifestyles and modern medicine seem to need. The issue of the right to choose to die is a particularly thorny one precisely because it remains something of a taboo, but it also challenges individuals to think about their own mortality. We don't want to accept that it will all, one day, end. By a very large margin, active supporters of right to die are people over fifty or those who are terminally ill or have a loved one who is. Consider the oddity of why the abortion rights controversy in America has remained for over half a century the big, hot-button political issue. Only a few women need that right when giving birth poses a problem for them. Most of those pontificating against abortion rights will never need the procedure. Yet we *all* die—but let's not think about that!

Another puzzle is why the right to die organizations in the US have such small memberships. Although around 50 percent of people in four states voted for a law permitting assistance in suicide, membership in Hemlock and other groups remained minuscule—forty thousand, tops. There is a willingness to use the secrecy of the ballot box, but to become a joiner and campaigner on this dicey issue seems not to go down well with friends and neighbors. Take Britain: numerous opinion surveys (including the government's own) have demonstrated that 80 percent of the population of 60 million wants law reform pertaining to the right to die issue. Nevertheless, membership of right to die groups (one of them is seventy years old) is under twenty thousand. Because the English churches, though poorly attended on Sundays, shout louder than this big segment of the population, the Parliament in London has eight times refused even modest changes in the choice in dying laws.

Therefore, it is still the case, by and large, that death by choice remains an outlawed, unmentionable subject—despite the facts that people are living longer but not necessarily (in their view) better lives, that modern medicine is now so sophisticated that a corpse can be ventilated, that degenerative diseases like Alzheimer's, ALS (the motor neuron disease), and multiple sclerosis now claim millions of victims, some of whom would prefer early release. Only the Swiss, Dutch, Belgians, and Oregonians have made positive reforms, and even those have limitations.

The reason I bond to the subject that I revived in 1980 with my books, and why I started Hemlock, is that I remain convinced that voluntary euthanasia (to use the word generically) is an inalienable civil liberty in a democratic society. We are unable to consider ourselves free people if we cannot consider the end.

How Will It Be for Me?

The question most asked of me by interviewers is: "How will you die?"

Obviously, I do not yet know the answer to that. Most in my family have died of a stroke. When and if I get such a blow, I hope it will kill me outright and not leave me in a semi-paralyzed limbo such as my mother and millions of other people have endured. If that happens, I hope somebody will have the mercy to quietly kill me, even if it has to be the traditional pillow over the face.

If my end fate is a terminal illness, I shall assess how it is affecting me and how long it might continue. If the pain management and quality of life are acceptable to me, then I shall stick it out to the natural close. I love life too much to waste any of it. If not, I shall advise those close to me that I shall shortly be bringing my life to a planned end. I might handle it myself or, of course, as a resident of Oregon, I could use the state's Death

With Dignity Act, which I helped to pass, for lawful physician-assisted suicide. As I've so often said, the aim is a good life and a good death.

APPENDIX

FOR FURTHER INFORMATION ON the issue of choices in dying, visit these websites:

www.finalexit.org
www.assistedsuicide.org
www.finalexit.org/ergo-store
www.finalexitnetwork.org
www.compassionandchoices.org
www.dyingwithdignity.org
www.worldrtd.net
https://en.wikipedia.org/wiki/Hemlock_Society
https://en.wikipedia.org/wiki/Jean's_Way
http://en.wikipedia.org/wiki/Derek_Humphry

LAW REFORMS UP TO 2016

Various forms of medical-assisted suicide have been approved in the following states and nations. Each law has its own limits, rules, and guidelines. All but Switzerland forbid foreigners this type of help to die. Only the Netherlands and Belgium permit chosen death via doctor's lethal injection—all others are by doctor prescription:

Switzerland 1940
Oregon 1994
Colombia 1997
The Netherlands 2002
Belgium 2002
Washington State 2008
Luxembourg 2009
Montana 2009 (court ruling only)
England and Wales 2010 (prosecution policy statement)
Vermont 2014
Quebec 2015
California 2015 (effective June 2016)
Canada 2016
Colorado 2016
Wash.DC 2017

ABOUT THE AUTHOR

A VETERAN JOURNALIST AND SUCCESSFUL author, **Derek Humphry** is regarded as the grand old man of the euthanasia movement, in which he remains deeply engaged, appearing frequently in major media. A dual citizen of the United States and the United Kingdom, he lives in Junction City, Oregon.

BOOKS BY DEREK HUMPHRY

General

Because They're Black (Martin Luther King Memorial Prize 1972)
Police Power and Black People Passports and Politics
The Cricket Conspiracy
False Messiah (with David Tindall)
Policing the Police (with Peter Hain)

Euthanasia

Jean's Way
Let Me Die Before I Wake
The Right to Die (with Ann Wickett)
Final Exit
Dying With Dignity
Freedom to Die (with Mary Clement)
The Good Euthanasia Guide
Good Life, Good Death (memoir)

Newspapers

Yorkshire Post (messenger)
Bristol Evening World
Manchester Evening News
London Daily Mail
Havering Recorder (editor)
London Sunday Times
Los Angeles Times